PALETTE
mini
PASTEL

Published and distributed by
viction:workshop ltd.

viction:ary™

viction:workshop ltd.
Unit C, 7/F, Seabright Plaza, 9-23 Shell Street,
North Point, Hong Kong SAR
Url: victionary.com
Email: we@victionary.com
 @victionworkshop
 @victionworkshop
Bē @victionary
 @victionary

Edited and produced by viction:ary

Creative direction by Victor Cheung
Book design by viction:workshop ltd.
Typeset in NB International Pro from Neubau

ISBN 978-988-79727-3-0
Printed and bound in China

5

PREFACE

According to the Cambridge Dictionary, the word 'palette' may refer to the range of colours that an artist usually paints with on a canvas. Today, however, more than just the primary means of creative expression for wielders of the physical brush, its role has expanded to include that of an important digital tool for crafting meaningful solutions in design. On top of manifesting pure works of the imagination as it has always done, the palette has become a purveyor of infinite visual possibilities with the power to bridge art and commerce. Since the release of its first edition in 2012, viction:ary's PALETTE colour-themed series has become one of the most successful and sought-after graphic design reference collections for students and working professionals around the world; showcasing a thoughtful curation of compelling ideas and concepts revolving around the palette featured. In keeping with the needs and wants of the savvy modern reader, the all-new PALETTE mini Series has been reconfigured and rejuvenated with fresh content, for all intents and purposes, to serve as the intriguing, instrumental, and timeless source of inspiration that its predecessor was, in a more convenient size.

INTRO

Once described as the favourite medium of master painters like Leonardo da Vinci, Michelangelo, Gauguin, and Monet, pastels are artist materials that offer an incredible range of colours and can be traced as far back to the Renaissance period when chalks were used for sketching. Although they are created using similar pigments to those found in other coloured arts media like oil paints, their milder tints stem from the neutral hue and low saturation of the binder used to hold the pigments together, diluting the latter's vibrancy. Ultimately, whatever physical form they may take, the soothing characteristics of pastels make them versatile shades to apply onto a variety of art and design projects.

It is not uncommon for people to associate the palette with traditionally feminine or child-like qualities due to its 'pure' and delicate nature; and depending on the mission or messages they want to convey, many brands embrace it to make an impression while connecting with their audiences on a deeper level. Therein lies its unique beauty, where its subtlety not only makes a strong statement on its own, but also invites viewers to scratch beyond the surface. For Mimigram, a mobile printing app from Russia that turns 'the best moments into awesome products' like photo collages, Veronica Levitskaya paired pastels with a modern logotype and graphic patterns to resonate with millennial women (PP. 108-115). She also created a Mimigram 'smiley face' to evoke the sense of happiness inherently tied in with the product. Similarly, Power-nap Over Design was inspired to use a pastel gradient to reflect the transition between the two opposing spectrums of one's innermost feelings (PP. 346-349). The Hong Kong-based studio's 'I'm Fine' single-use camera was inspired by the answer people typically give when they are asked 'how are you?' – one that many use as a 'smokescreen' to cover up their actual thoughts and emotions – as well as the fine texture of the film loaded.

For designers who enjoy the challenge of changing perspectives or trying something new, the palette is a striking means to push creative boundaries. In updating the studio's own branding, Raw Color fused colour, material, and tactility into a unique system that highlighted its design offerings in a flexible way (PP. 022-025). It chose five different shades from a blend of two PMS swatches to produce varying intensities that it then applied to various communication materials to connote endless possibilities. For the 2013 edition of the Eastern Electrics Festival, the biggest outdoor celebration of underground house and techno, Bunch based its work on paler tones instead of the louder ones typically associated with the music genres and party scene (PP. 032-039). By turning the festival's visual language on its head, the studio found a clever means to update the use of pastels. Likewise, Studio Spass contrasted simple pastel shapes against a black backdrop to create eye-catching collaterals for West Side Stories, an architecture festival that comprised an exhibition, lectures, and a publication (PP. 450-457). Drawn to the post-modern aesthetics of Rotterdam's golden age of urban renewal, the studio highlighted the muted hues in a stark manner that deemed them hard to ignore.

With shades like light azure, creamy mint, and whimsy yellow, it can be difficult to take pastels seriously due to their effortless charm (and their names alone) at first. However, when wielded properly and expertly combined with other design elements, they make for powerful secret weapons that disarm the viewer and add a distinct character to any final outcome.

ASTRID ORTIZ
DIRECCIÓN DE ARTE Y DISEÑO GRÁFICO
Tel. 645 78 94 38 | hola@astridortiz.com
Casanova 57, 6 - 4 08011 Barcelona
www.astridortiz.com

ASTRID
DIRECCIÓN DE AR
Tel. 645 78 94
Casanova

ASTRID ORTIZ
DIRECCIÓN DE ARTE Y DISEÑO GRÁFICO
Tel. 645 78 94 38 | hola@astridortiz.com
Casanova 57, 6 - 4 08011 Barcelona
www.astridortiz.com

ASTRID ORTIZ
DIRECCIÓN DE ARTE Y DISEÑO GRÁF
Tel. 645 78 94 38 | hola@astri
Casanova 57, 6 - 4 08011
www.astrid

ASTRID ORTIZ
DIRECCIÓN DE ARTE Y DISEÑO GRÁFICO
Tel. 645 78 94 38 | hola@astridortiz.com
Casanova 57, 6 - 4 08011 Barcelona
www.astridortiz.com

ASTRID ORTIZ
DIRECCIÓN DE ARTE Y DISEÑO GRÁFICO
Tel. 645 78 94 38 | hola@astridortiz.com
Casanova 57, 6 - 4 08011 Barcelona
www.astridortiz.com

OSCAR ESPINOSA
Diseñador 3d

tel. (+52) 123 45 67 89
hello@oscarespinosa.com
www.oscarespinosa.com

OSCAR ES
Diseñ

tel. (
hello@
www

OSCAR ESPINOSA
Diseñador 3d

tel. 651 02 37 57
hello.a.oscarespinosa.com
www.oscarespinosa.com

OSCAR ESPINOSA
Diseñador 3d

tel. 651 02 37 57
hello.a.oscarespinosa.com
www.oscarespinosa.com

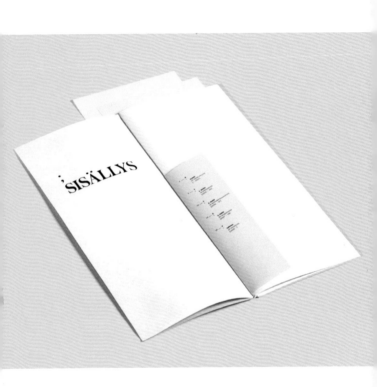

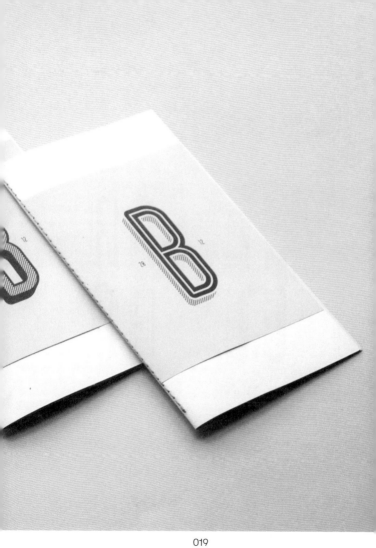

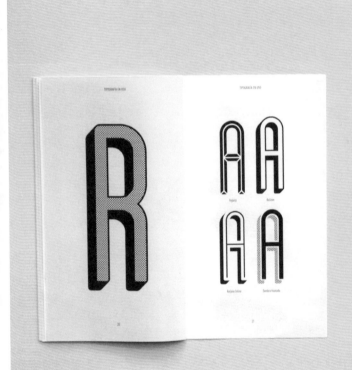

ABCDEFGHIJKL
MNOPQRS
TUVWXYZ
0123456789
.,:;()[]+=-\&
'¡!@€¿?ÇÑ%

Blanch Caps

318
VARIETATS

Blanch Condensed Light 270 pt

Blanch Condensed Heavy 79 pt

PERA BLANQUILLA, PRÈSSEC GROC, POMA FUJI,
TOMÀQUET, PERA LLIMONERA, POMA GOLDEN,
POMA ROYAL GALA, PRÈSSEC GROC,

Blanch Caps 14 pt

RAW
COLOR

pidan

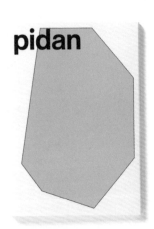

pidan

pic

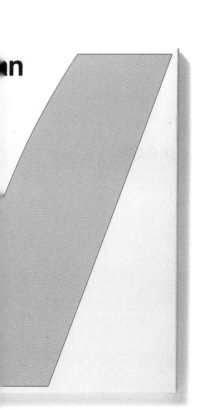

pidan

Pet shovel
Pelle à litière
猫砂スコップ
猫砂铲

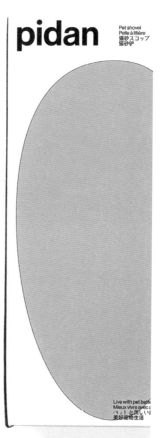

Live with pet better
Mieux vivre avec
パットと優しい
美好宠物生活

pidan

n

pidan Pet toy
Jouet pour animaux domestiques
ペットおもちゃ
寵物玩具

Richie Hawtin-Saturday

Masters At Work-Sunday

Maya Jane Coles-Friday

EASTERNELECTRICS.COM

Camping options
3 Day weekend Camping—£115
3 Day Weekend VIP Camping—£180
Fri. + Sat. Tickets—£80
Sat. + Sun. Tickets—£70

Day Tickets
Fri. Single Day Ticket—£40
Sat. Single Day Ticket—£45
Sun. Single Day Ticket—£30
VIP Single Day Tickets
available from £60

All tickets available at
easternelectrics.com

Eastern Electrics
Festival
2–4 August
Knebworth Park

EASTERNELECTRICS.COM

Over 100 of the world's
finest house and techno
acts including...

Eastern Electrics
Festival
2–4 August
Knebworth Park

Knebworth, Hertfordshire
40 minutes from Central London

EASTERNELECTRICS.COM

Eastern Electrics
Festival
2–4 August
Knebworth Park

Ben UFO
Blawan
Joy Orbison

+ 100 more of the world's finest underground house and techno acts

easternelectrics.com

EASTERNELECTRICS.COM

Eastern Electrics
Festival
2—4 August
Knebworth Park

The UK's biggest outdoor celebration of underground house and techno

easternelectrics.com

EASTERNELECTRICS.COM

Don't miss the UK's biggest celebration of underground house and techno!

Day tickets from £30!
£115 weekend camping tickets almost gone!
Standard tickets £145

Eastern Electrics
Festival
2–4 August
Knebworth Park

EASTERNELECTRICS.COM

Don't miss the UK's biggest celebration of underground house and techno!

Day tickets from £30!
£115 weekend camping tickets almost gone!
Standard tickets £145

Eastern Electrics
Festival
2–4 August
Knebworth Park

EASTERNELECTRICS.COM

Eastern Electrics
Festival
2–4 August
Knebworth Park

Richie Hawtin
Hot Natured
feat. Jamie Jones
Lee Foss, Luca C
& Ali Love
Maceo Plex
Masters At Work
Maya Jane Cole
Seth Troxler

"Boasting one of the strongest
dance lineups around"
–Time Out

Claude Von Stroke
Damian Lazarus
Deetron
Dixon
DJ Sneak
Dyed Soundorom
Eats Everything
Ellen Allien
Francesca Lombardo
Guy Gerber
Heidi
Huxley
Joy Orbison
Kerri Chandler
Laura Jones
Magda
Matthias Tanzmann
Maxxi Soundsystem

MK
Miguel Campbell
Nick Curly
No Artificial Colours
PBR Streetgang
Raresh
Richy Ahmed
Ryan Crosson
Sasha
Shaun Reeves
Skream
Soul Bros: Soul Clap
+ The Martinez Brothers
Tale Of Us
Subben
tINI
Waifs&Strays
+ much more

EASTERNELECTRICS.COM

Eastern Electrics
Festival
2–4 August
Knebworth Park

Seth Troxler
Maya Jane Coles
Maceo Plex

Day tickets from £30!
£115 weekend camping tickets almost gone!
Standard tickets £145

(e)

EASTERNELECTRICS.COM

IGLOOVISION STAGE

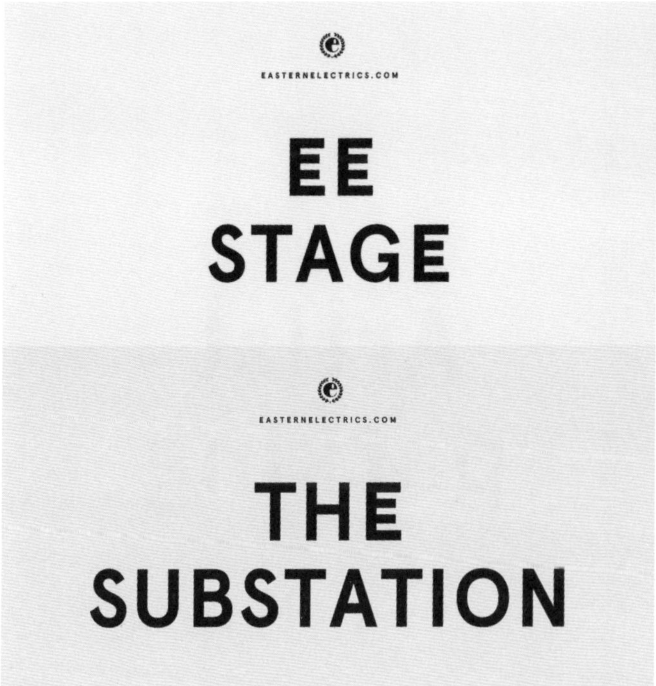

(e)

EASTERNELECTRICS.COM

EE STAGE

(e)

EASTERNELECTRICS.COM

THE SUBSTATION

Eastern Electrics Festival 2013

Artist parking

Eastern Electrics Festival 2013

Eastern Electrics Festival 2013

Disabled parking

Traders

Eastern Electrics Festival 2013

Eastern Electrics Festival 2013

Static vehicle

On site moving vehicle

Spring
Summer
13

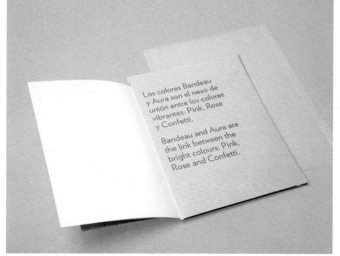

Los colores Bandeau
y Aura son el nexo de
unión entre los colores
vibrantes: Pink, Rose
y Confetti.

Bandeau and Aura are
the link between the
bright colours: Pink,
Rose and Confetti.

QT RESORT

87 - 109 Port Douglas Road,
Port Douglas QLD 4877 Australia
Phone +61 7 4099 8900
www.qtportdouglas.com.au

ROOM No.

—
QT RESORT

87–109 Port Douglas Road
Port Douglas QLD 4877 Australia
Phone: +61 7 4099 8900
www.qtportdouglas.com.au

ROOM No.

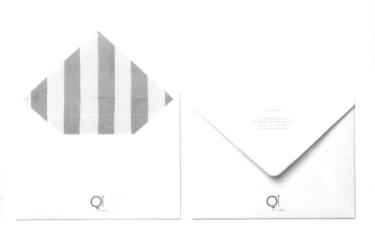

QT RESORT

ESTILO

PORT DOUGLAS

67-109 PORT DOUGLAS ROAD
PORT DOUGLAS QLD 4877 AUSTRALIA
PHONE. +61 7 4099 8900
WWW.QTPORTDOUGLAS.COM.AU

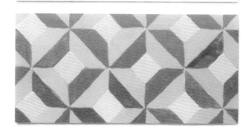

"Pastel colours have the ability to add variety and keep viewers in high spirits."

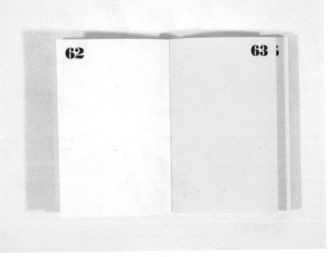

365

62

63 5

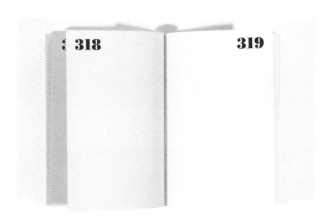

非道
園子温

芸術実行
Chim↑

「

情報（
津田

極端だから、人をひきつける。

情報の呼吸法
津田大介

idea
ink
01

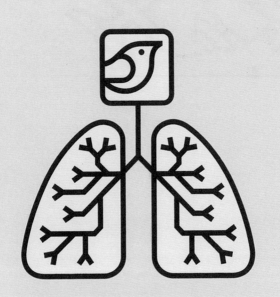

発信しなければ、得るものはない。

芸術実行犯
Chim↑Pom （チン↑ポム）

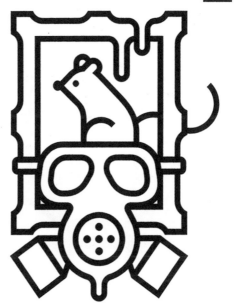

アートが新しい自由をつくる。

世界婚活
中村綾花

idea
ink
06

恋愛のガラパゴスから抜け出す。

外食2.0
君島佐和子

idea
ink
05

外食は「おいしさ」の先を目指す。

ソーシャルデザイン

—— 社会をつくるグッドアイデア集

グリーンズ編

idea ink

02

社会の問題は、楽しく解決できる。

非道に生きる
園子温

極端だから、人をひきつける。

MALE : MALE RATIO
THE DESIGN FIELD

FEMALE : MALE RATIO
IN THE DESIGN FIELD

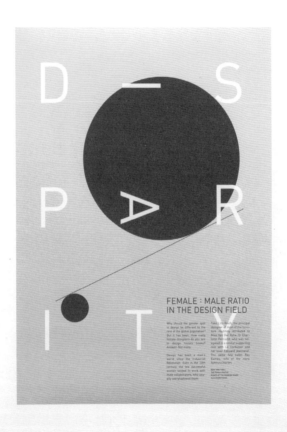

D—S

P A R

I T Y

FEMALE : MALE RATIO
IN THE DESIGN FIELD

Why should the gender split in design be different to the rest of the global population? But it has been. How really female designers do you see in design, history books? Answer: Not many.

Design has been a man's world since the Industrial Revolution. Even in the 20th century the few successful women landed in work with male collaborators, who usually overshadowed them.

Take Lilly Reich, the principal designer of much of the furniture routinely attributed to Mies Van Der Rohe. Or Charlotte Perriand, who was relegated to a minor supporting role with Le Corbusier and her lover Edouard Jeanneret. The same fate befell Ray Eames, wife of the more famous Charles.

NEW YORK TIMES
THE FEMALE FACTOR
WOMEN OF THE BAUHAUS SHARE
HALLIE EVERSTINE

FEMALE : MALE RATIO IN THE DESIGN FIELD

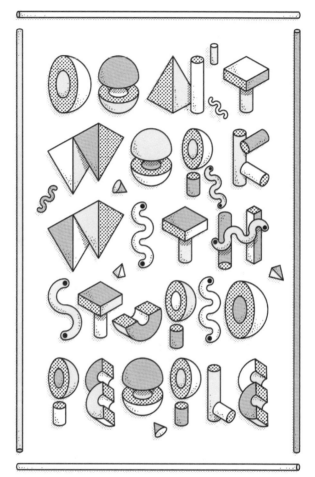

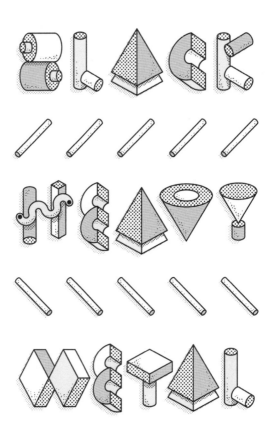

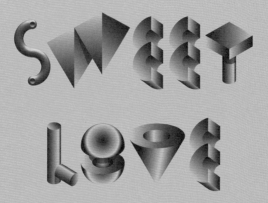

073

FIRST ANNUAL
DVA SEMINAR
—ROBERT
MARSHALL

FORMER
FACULTY
MEMBER OF
STUDIO/
PAINTING
AREA

ALL STUDENTS ARE INVITED
TO ATTEND THE FIRST
ANNUAL DEPARTMENT WIDE
DVA SEMINAR

FEB. 16

11 AM—12 NOON

MADSEN
RECITAL HALL

REFRESHMENTS
TO FOLLOW THE
LECTURE

FOR MORE INFORMATION PLEASE CONTACT THE DVA SECRETARIES IN H-FAC E-509

DVA

FIRST ANNUAL
DVA SEMINAR
—ROBERT
MARSHALL

FORMER
FACULTY
MEMBER OF
STUDIO/
PAINTING
AREA

ALL STUDENTS ARE INVITED
TO ATTEND THE FIRST
ANNUAL DEPARTMENT WIDE
DVA SEMINAR

FEB. 16

11 AM—12 NOON

REFRESHMENTS
TO FOLLOW THE
LECTURE

MADSEN
RECITAL HALL

FOR MORE INFORMATION PLEASE CONTACT THE DVA SECRETARIES IN H-FAC E-509

DVA

POLA MUSEUM ANNEX

TaikoMatsuo_
Layered

リズム豊かな配色、
不思議な錯覚を生むフレーム構成で、
観る者の心を奪い続けている松尾たいこ。

広告や雑誌、ファッションブランドとのコラボレーションなど幅広くイラストを描きつづけている彼女だが、本の装丁画には特に定評がある。『クライマーズ・ハイ』(文春文庫)、『日本の古典をよむ』シリーズ(小学館)など、これまで手がけてきたのは250冊以上。彼女の作品は、さまざまなレイヤーを持ち名の魅力を放つ。
それは"絵を決定づけるモチーフの配置、あるいは色調が重層的"ということだが、"原画にテキストのレイヤーが重なって世に出る"という作品の使われ方の特徴とも言える。そのような意味を抽出して名付けられた本展では、これまで描き続けてきた数千点にも及ぶ作品からセレクトした原画に加え、新作を発表。山や森、そこに駆け巡る兎と鹿、鳥や犬が見せる愛しさなどを表現した作品が、幾層にも折り重なる。そんな壁に身を置くと、心にある穏やかな気持ちが笑と共鳴し、翳るない、そして新しい世界を体感することができるだろう。

松尾たいこ/イラストレーター
広島県生まれ。第3回ザ・チョイス年度賞 鈴木成一賞を受賞。著作に絵本『空が見かったこと』や作曲者大月みなこ氏の作品「Presents」、「なくしたものたちの街」がある。これまで250冊以上の装幀画を手がけているが、広告、CDジャケット、雑誌、ファッションブランドやミュージアムショップにも作品を提供するなど幅広い分野で活躍。アジアを中心に海外での評価も高い。
http://taikomatsuo.jimdo.com

TaikoMatsuo_
Layered

2011年4月22日(金)〜5月29日(日)

11:00〜20:00(入場は閉場の30分前まで)/会期中無休/入場無料
主　催／ポーラ ミュージアム アネックス
会場構成／porastyle
企画協力／midi
企画制作／PARCO
お問合せ／03-3563-5501(ポーラ ミュージアム アネックス)

ポーラ ミュージアム アネックス

東京都中央区銀座1-7-7 ポーラ銀座ビル3F 〒104-0061

TaikoMatsuo_
Layered

PARCO出版

A4判変型/50ページ/2,520円(税込)
6月1日一般発売(会場にて先行発売決定)

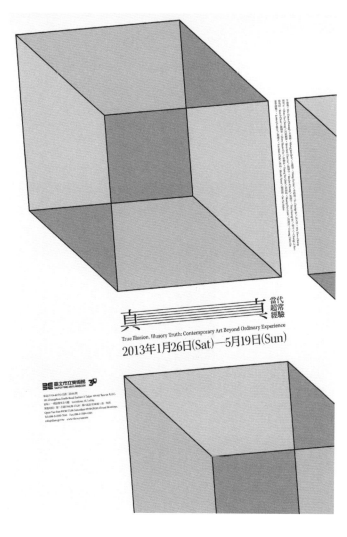

真　　　　　真　當代
　　　　　　　　　　超常
　　　　　　　　　　經驗

True Illusion, Illusory Truth: Contemporary Art Beyond Ordinary Experience

2013年1月26日(Sat)—5月19日(Sun)

臺北市立美術館 3F

臺北/104-632臺北市中山北路三段181號
181 Zhongshan North Road Section 3 Taipei 104-632 Taiwan R.O.C.
開放時間：週二至週日09:30-17:30 週六延長至20:30 週一休館
Open Tue-Sun 09:30-17:30, Saturdays 09:30-20:30 Closed Mondays.
Tel: 886-2-2595-7656　Fax: 886-2-2594-4104
info@tfam.gov.tw　www.tfam.museum

SPRING SUMMER
2012

The Modern Diary Collection

03 The Massimo Dutti Accessories.

05 The Massimo Dutti Boys & Girls' Collectio

02 The Massimo Dutti Men's Collection.

01 The Massimo Dutti Women's Collection.

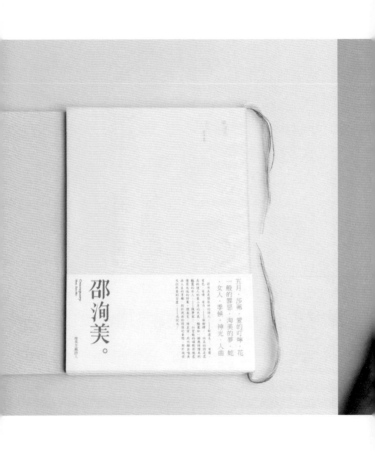

五月・莎霏・爱的叮咛・花
一般的罪恶・洵美的梦・蛇
女人・季候・神光・人曲

邵洵美。

那樹帳內草褥上的甘露，

正像新婚夜處女的蜜淚……

又如浮婦上下體的沸汗，

能使多少顫魂日夜罪迷。

rdals

Art Direction

Eksponeringsdesign

Film & TV

Grafisk design

Tekst & skribent

Scenografi & event

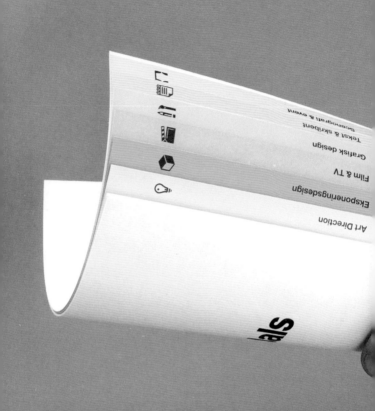

Art Direction

Eksponeringsdesign

Film & TV

Grafisk design

Tekst & skribent

scenografi & event

als

"You can use [pastels] in abundance without making the result too saturated."

Art Direction

Som Art Director blir du
visuell leder og konsept-
utvikler av høy kvalitet.

Film & TV

Som film & tv-utdannet
arbeider du med historie-
fortelling, regi og produk-
sjon for film, web og ulike
tv-formater.

MIDDLE OF NOWHERE

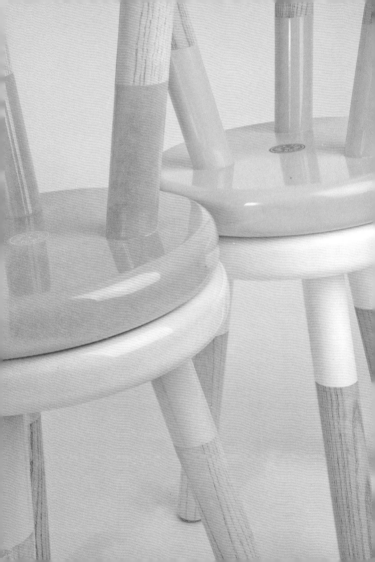

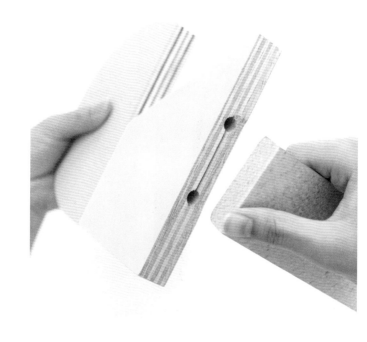

104

IN JEDEM STECKT EIN ANDERER, DEN WIR NICHT KENNEN

Drogen eröffnen den Zugang zu unseren unbewussten Schaltkreisen. Dass jeder in seinem einen Anderen hat, den man nicht kennt, haben schon früh Schriftsteller wie Goethe oder William Blake durch Opium am eigenen Leib erfahren – ihre Werte wurden durch eine unsichtbare Macht beeinflusst. Dieser Wirkung gegenüber sind wir vollkommen machtlos, denn manche Drogen wirken wie ein Schlüssel-Schloss-System manipulativ auf uns ein. Sie könnten sich in das neuronale Schaltsystem des Organismus ein, das für Belohnungssystem zuständig ist. Das Resultat ist der Eindruck des Paradies zu erfahren.

Das Hirn arbeitet auf zu leisten, weil weg von unserem Bewusstsein und präsentiert das fertige Endprodukt, die geniale Idee, den gewaltigen Gedankengang. Dem gebührt der Rufen für geniale Ideen, wenn unser Gehirn uns unbewusst, aber inbegriffen, steuert?

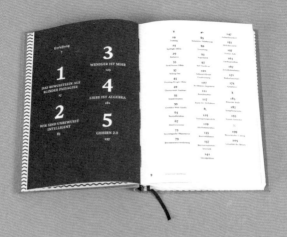

hoi bo /

CARE

To clean, simply wipe with a damp cloth. When not in use for long periods, the wax can develop a natural white bloom. This is perfectly normal and will go away with use. You can also use a blow dryer to gently warm the bag and the bloom will disappear.

HOIBO.COM

INFLUENCIA

LA REVUE
DE LA COMMUNICATION
ET DES TENDANCES

N°7

Octobre / décembre 2013
25 €

LA CULTURE

UNE INVITÉE
DE(S)
MARQUE(S)

INFLUENCIA.NET

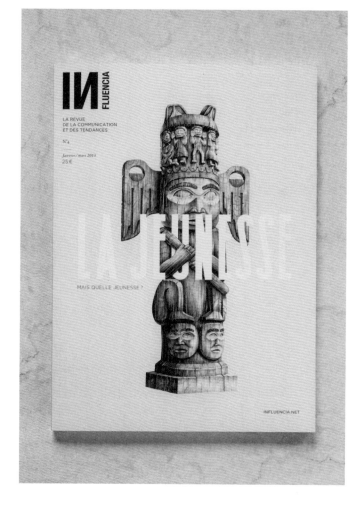

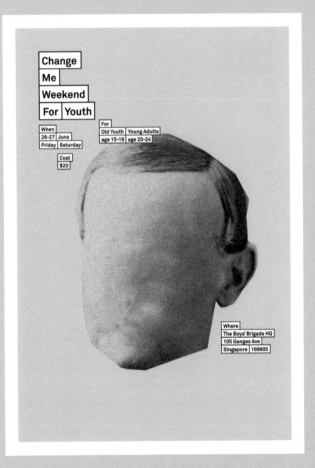

Change
Me
Weekend
For Youth

When
26-27 June
Friday Saturday

For
Old Youth Young Adults
age 15-19 age 20-24

Cost
$20

Where
The Boys' Brigade HQ
105 Ganges Ave
Singapore 169605

Change Me Weekend For Youth

Where
The Boys' Brigade HQ
105 Ganges Ave
Singapore | 169605

When
26-27 | June
Friday | Saturday

Cost
$20

For
Old Youth | Young Adults
age 15-19 | age 20-24

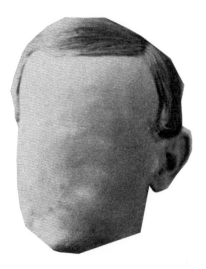

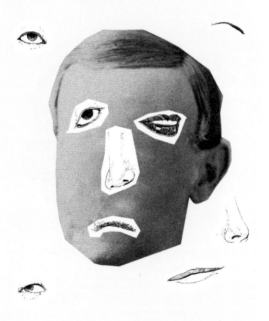

Change Me Weekend For Youth

Where
The Boys' Brigade HQ
105 Ganges Ave
Singapore | 169605

When
26-27 | June
Friday | Saturday

Cost
$20

For
Old Youth | Young Adults
age 15-19 | age 20-24

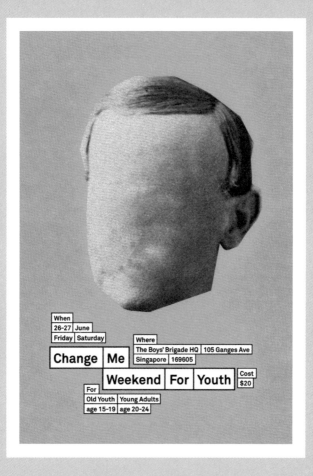

When
26-27 June
Friday Saturday

Change Me

Weekend For Youth

Where
The Boys' Brigade HQ | 105 Ganges Ave
Singapore | 169605

Cost
$20

For
Old Youth | Young Adults
age 15-19 | age 20-24

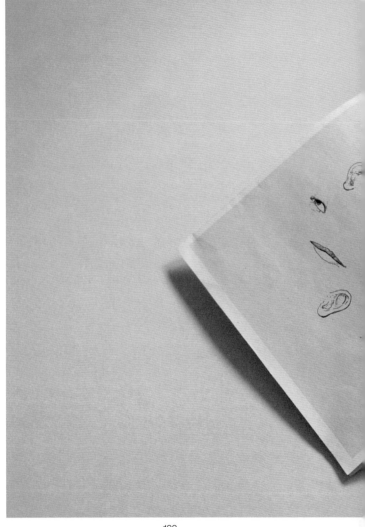

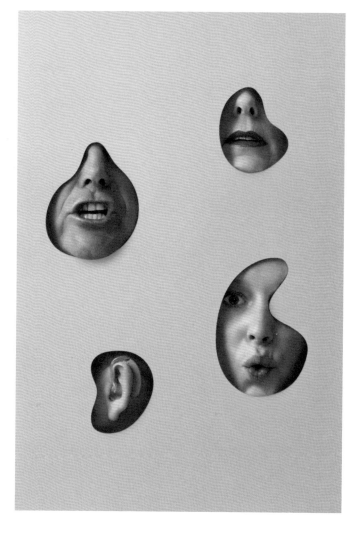

TRIBES

NINA RAINE

silotheatre.co.nz

"Pastels look the best when they are produced by Nature, like the dusk of a very hot day which varies in neon pastel."

145

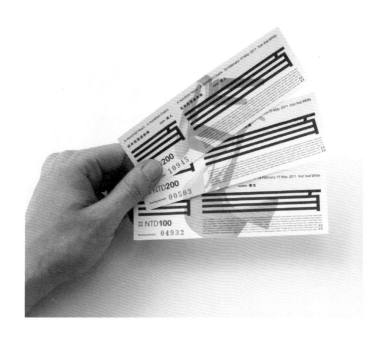

RAKKAUDESTA

HELSINKI
FOOD
COMPANY

RUOKAAN

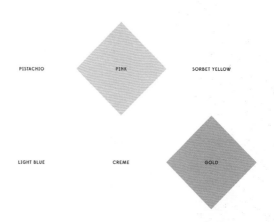

PISTACHIO   PINK   SORBET YELLOW

LIGHT BLUE   CREME   GOLD

HELSINKI ◇ WWW.HELSINKIFOODCOMPANY.FI

JOHANNA LINDHOLM +358 (0)40 8308973
HANNA.LINDHOLM@HELSINKIFOODCOMPANY.FI

RAKKAUDESTA

HELSINKI FOOD COMPANY

RUOKAAN

HELSINKI FOOD COMPANY ⋄ RIKHARDINKATU 4 B 14, 00130 HELSINKI ⋄ WWW.HELSINKIFOODCOMPANY.FI
TERESA VÄLIMÄKI +358 (0)40 8260622   JOHANNA LINDHOLM +358 (0)40 8308973
TERESA.VALIMAKI@HELSINKIFOODCOMPANY.FI   JOHANNA.LINDHOLM@HELSINKIFOODCOMPANY.FI

152

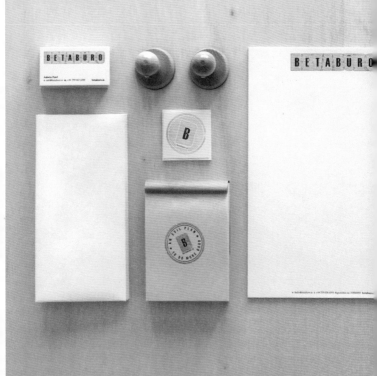

154

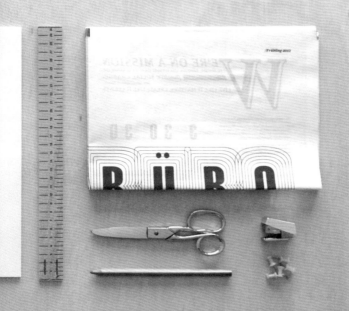

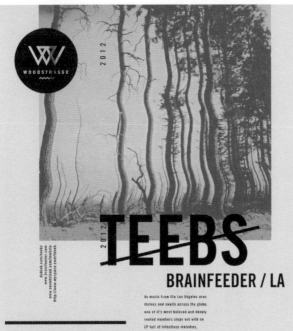

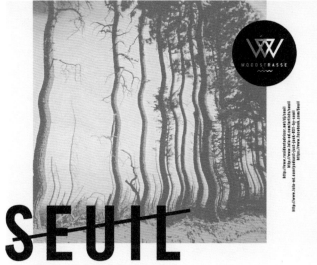

WOODSTRASSE

2012

2012

SEUIL

EKLO, HOLD YOUTH /FR

For this second edition at M.Wong
we welcome the talented, great DJ
and authentic producer, SEUIL, who
brought us during the past years
some hi level releases on hot
imprints like EKLO, FREAK N CHIC,
HOLD YOUTH, MINIBAR, MOON

october

30.10.2012

@ MR WONG   Zwarte Lievevrouwstraat 11,
1000 Brussels,
Belgium

WOOD
STRASSE
TREE
HUGGERS

design: koozi.com

SEUIL

EKLO, HOLD YOUTH /FR

For this second edition of W.Wong
we welcome the talented, great DJ
and authentic producer, SEUIL, who
brought us during the past years
some hi level releases on hot
imprints like EKLO, FREAK N CHIC,
HOLD YOUTH, MINIBAG, MOON.

october

30.10.2012

@ MR WONG Zwarte Lieuwenbewstraat 14,
1000 Brussels,
Belgium.

WOOD
STRASSE
TREE
HUGGERS

2012

2012

WOODSTRASSE

2012

CHYMERA

OVUM/NRK/DELSIN/BERLIN

Chymera was born and raised in
Ireland, but currently resides in
Berlin. He creates a unique mix of
techno and house, occasionally
touching on electronica, electro and
ambient, for such renowned labels
as Ovum, NRK, Delsin and others. He
is in demand on the DJ and Live
circuit and has played all over
Europe, Asia, Australia and North
AmericaHARBOUR, LESSIZMORE,
CIRCUS COMPANY

november

25.11.2012

WOOD
STRASSE
TREE
HUGGERS

@ MR WONG Zwarte Lievevrouwstraat 14,
1000 Brussels,
Belgium

2012

PRESS
OFFICES
AROUND
THE
WORLD

PULL&BEAR

PULL&BEAR

SS2012
TRENDS

MEN'S LOOKBOOK

PULL&BEAR

PULL&BEAR

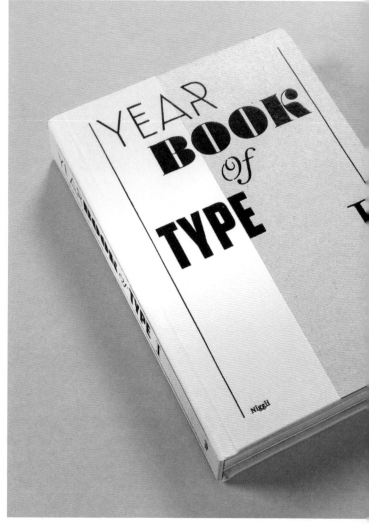

Edited by Slanted

Sans Serif

Essays & Tutorials
Designing a Typeface

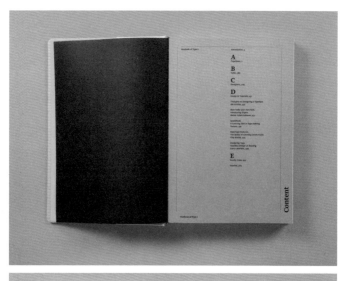

Descobreix el gran
mercat del fresc

Visites
Navegant entre enigmes
El futur està en joc
Enigma Omega-3

Inscriu-te!
mercabarna.es/visitesinsolites

Mercabarna t'obre les portes perquè
coneguis el gran mercat del fresc.
Tria una de les nostres visites insòlites,
que combinen aventura i gastronomia.
No t'ho perdis!

mercabarna

MERCABARNA
VISITES INSÒLITES

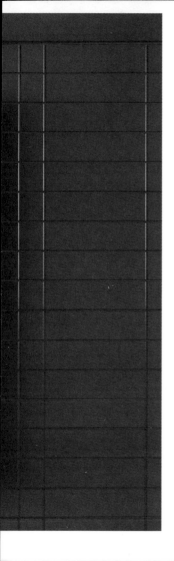

MERCA
VISITES IN

MERCABARNA
VISITES INSÒLITES

Enigma Omega-3
Nit de cuina i misteri
al mercat del peix

mercabarna

de fruites
alisses

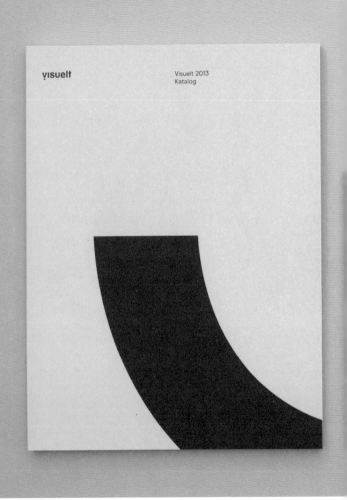

visuelt

Visuelt 2013
Katalog

s 97

TANK
NÄR ⊕
TOXIC®

Scandinavian
Designgroup

Arrangert av Grafill,
Norsk organisasjon for
visuell kommunikasjon

visuelt

Open Studio Crawl:
Visuelt 2013 — where
the magic happens!

A NEW CODE FOR THE MIDTOWN

Thank You!
¡GRACIAS!

Designed for those who believe there is
more that what they have; that life must
...by the sea,
...alm trees.

You will find
how easy life
becomes

WHEN LIVING AT IPANA

Smartas.—bath tissue

we learn as we go

Luxury Bath Tissue
Papier Toilette de Luxe
Papel Higiénico de Lujo

Smartas. —bath tissue

we learn as we go

Luxury Bath Tissue
Papier Toilette de Luxe
Papel Higiénico de Lujo

189

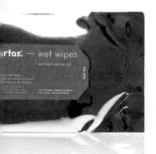

WE ARE ALL IN THIS TOGETHER

WE ARE ALL IN THIS **TOGETHER**

THE FOLDED PAPER COLLECTION
ITEM N°02

THE FOLDED PAPER COLLECTION
ITEM N°03

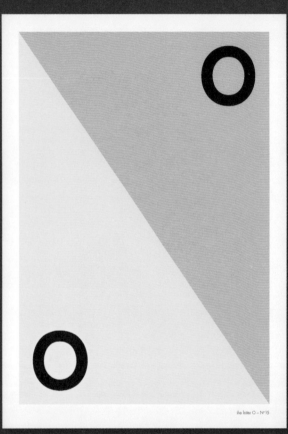

the letter O – N°15

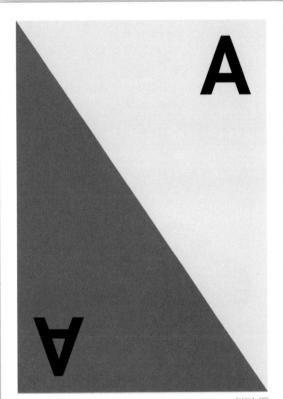

the letter A – Nº01

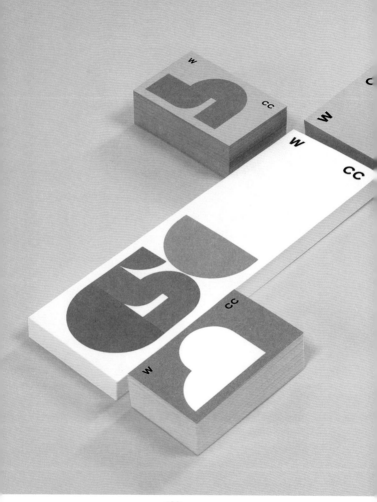

198

intuitive intent

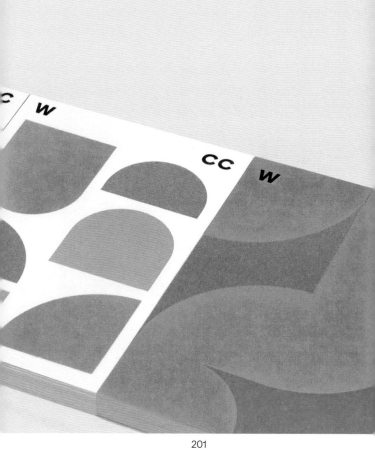

202

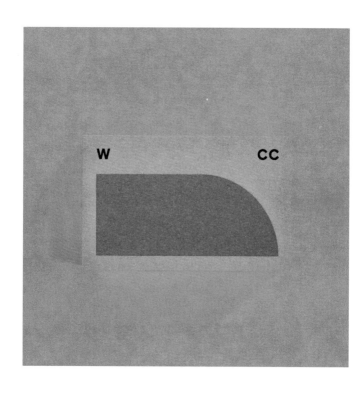

INFUSIÓNES NATURALES
(MANZANA E HIGO)
—
BÔNNARD
BÔUTIQUE DE REPÔSTERÍA Y TÉ

1886 · 2658

Té Negro

Se caracteriza por su sabor robusto y definido. Puedes disfrutarte
notas cremosas, condimentadas, ligeramente florales y herbales.
Son excelentes para levantarse por la mañana y relajantes
naturales por la tarde. Es perfecto para combinarse
con endulzante y leche.

Manzana de Nueva Inglaterra en combinación con higos dulces.
Contiene ligeros toques de clavo y de anís que realzan la dulzura
del té. Es una mezcla versátil que sabe muy bien helado, caliente
o con un toque ligero de whisky para consentir el alma.
Ingredientes: Té negro, té oolong, moóbos orgánicos,
manzana, higo, clavo y anís.

Empacado por Tea Guys, LLC.

WWW.BONNARD.COM.MX

NET WT 4.0 oz (114g) 30-40 PORCIONES

INFUSIÓNES NATURALES
(MANZANILLA CON VAINILLA)
—
BÔNNARD
BÔUTIQUE DE REPÔSTERÍA Y TÉ

1886 · 2658

Té Herbal y Frutal

Hechas con los mejores ingredientes que la naturaleza puede
ofrecer, flores, semillas, granos y frutas. Todas las mezclas herbales
están naturalmente libres de cafeína. Perfectamente adecuado
para tomarse a cualquier hora del día, calientes o frías.

La fina mezcla de té de manzanilla con vainilla y citronella logran
un té balanceado. Excelente opción para tomar antes de dormir.
Ingredientes: Manzanilla, arbusto de miel orgánico,
hinhicho, citronella, regaliz, vaina de vainilla,
hoja de stevia y uvas.

Empacado por Tea Guys, LLC.

WWW.BONNARD.COM.MX

NET WT 4.0 oz (114g) 30-40 PORCIONES

INFUSIÓNES NATURALES
(SPA PURIFICANTE)
—
BÔNNARD
BÔUTIQUE DE REPÔSTERÍA Y TÉ

KSPE 1001

Té Spa

Combinación de té purificantes, energizantes y relajantes.
Invitan a tomarse un momento y disfrutar de los beneficios de
esta mezcla de aromas suaves y delicados.

Mezcla antioxidante de rooibos, honeybush, bayas de enebro,
caléndula y hojas de abedul. Este té ayuda a mantener el sistema
inmunológico saludable y a deshacerse de las toxinas que se
acumulan diariamente. Disfrútalo caliente o frío.
Ingredientes: Rooibos orgánico, arbusto de miel orgánico,
limón mirto, jugo de limón, enebro, jengibre,
raíz de regaliz, anís, citronella, caléndula, stevia,
hojas de abedul y corteza de sauce blanco.

Empacado por Tea Guys, LLC.

WWW.BONNARD.COM.MX

NET WT 4.0 oz (114₂) 30-40 PORCIONES

INFUSIÓNES NATURALES
(MANGO Y PÉTALOS DE ROSA)
—
BÔNNARD
BÔUTIQUE DE REPÔSTERÍA Y TÉ

KSPT 1001

Té Verde

Sabor ligero y delicado con cualidades de hierbas y vegetales.
Rico en Vitamina C y antioxidantes, el té verde es conocido
por sus beneficios a la salud. Esta mezcla de té sobrepasa
todas las expectativas.

Exótica mezcla de té verde, té blanco y el oolong con exuberante
mango y rosas amarillas que logran un bouquet frutal y saludable.
Ideal para compartir con tus amigos en el atardecer.
Naturalmente bajo en cafeína.
Ingredientes: Té verde orgánico, té blanco, té oolong,
mango, rosa y pétalos de varias flores.

Empacado por Tea Guys, LLC.

WWW.BONNARD.COM.MX

NET WT 4.0 oz (114₂) 30-40 PORCIONES

PÂTISSERIE
(À BIENTÔT)
—
BÔNNARD
BÔUTIQUE DE REPÔSTERÍA Y TÉ

EST. 2011

MACARONS
(À BIENTÔT)
—
BÔNNARD
BÔUTIQUE DE REPÔSTERÍA Y TÉ

EST. 2011

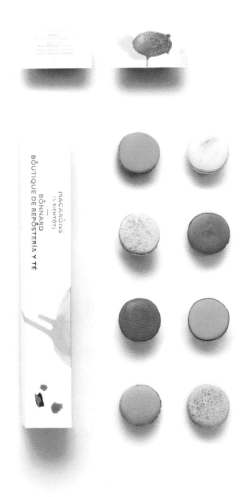

INFUSIÕNES NATURALES
(MANZANA E HIGO)
—
BÓNNARD
BÒUTIQUE DE REPÓSTERÍA Y TÉ

Té Negro

Se caracteriza por su sabor robusto y definido. Pueden disfrutarse
notas cremosas, condimentadas, ligeramente florales y herbales.
Son excelentes para levantarse por la mañana y relajarse
saturada por la tarde. Es perfecto para combinarse
con endulzante y leche.

Manzana de Nueva Inglaterra en combinación con higos dulces.
Contiene ligeros toques de clavo y de anís que realzan la dulzura
del té. En una mezcla versátil que sabe muy bien helada, caliente
o con un toque ligero de whisky para consentir el alma.
Ingredientes: Té negro, té oolong, rooibos orgánico,
manzana, higo, clavo y anís.

Empacado por Tex Guys, LLC.
WWW.BONNARD.COM.MX

NET WT 4.0 oz (114g) 38-40 PORCIONES

211

"[Pastels] can add a lovely sense of sophistication to the overall design when the palette is expanded, especially as a design backdrop."

Invitation

서울일러스트레이션페어 W 2018

12.28.FRI. — 31.MON

**The Seoul
Illustration Fair**

주최
오씨에이커스

협찬
네이버
CRAFOLIO

미디어파트너
디자인프레스
designrace

W

The Seoul Illustration Fair W

서울일러스트레이션페어W2018
The Seoul Illustration Fair W 2018
12.28.FRI   31.MON.
COEX B Hall

(우)08023
서울시 양천구 신월로 389, 남부빌딩 8층, 813호
서울일러스트레이션페어 사무국 (주)오에배어스
T 02-2082-8601

초대권 제공

12.28.FRI.
— 31.MON.
COEX B Hall

주최
오메페이퍼스
협찬
그라폴리오
GRAFOLIO
티자인위에인
디자인진위에인
designmine

...airw.co.kr

...oul Illustration Fair   W

...어W 2018

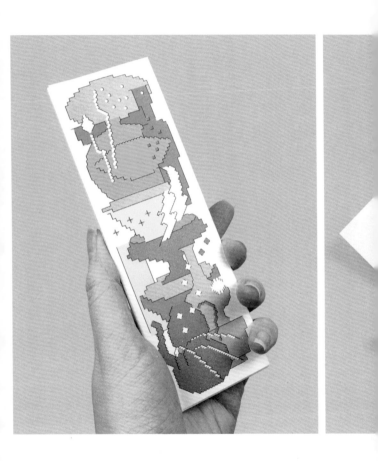

219

220

222

223

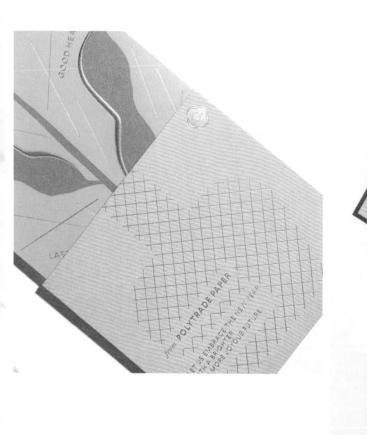

GOOD HEA

LAST

from POLYTRADE PAPER

LET US EMBRACE THE NEW YEAR
WITH A BRIGHTER
A MORE JOYOUS FUTURE.

HOPE THE DAYS A[...] ARE FILLED W[...]

from **POLYTRADE PAPER**

LET US EMBRACE THE NEW YEAR
WITH A BRIGHTER
AND MORE JOYOUS FUTURE

228

LASTING PROSPER

GOOD HEALTH

from POLYTRADE PAPER

LET US EMBRACE THE NEW YEAR
WITH A BRIGHTER
AND MORE JOYOUS FUTURE

229

DOUBLE FLAVOURS

125 g/克
杯裝或筒裝
CUP OR CONE

MOP35

Gelato Cake
$120 禮券
Assorted Gelato & Cake

LemonCello

LemonCello
檸檬車露

230

DAILY & FRESH MADE IN MACAU

$30 贈券

Assorted Gelato & Cake

Gelato Cake

LemonCello
檸檬車露

Big Part

Hire Me 歡迎預約

LemonCello®
檸檬車露

232

234

235

THEATRE ACADEMY
UNIVERSITY OF THE ARTS HELSINKI

SIBELIUS ACADEMY
UNIVERSITY OF THE ARTS HELSINKI

THEATRE ACADEMY

TUOMAS AUVINEN
Dean, Ph.D., EMBA
SIBELIUS ACADEMY
UNIVERSITY OF THE ARTS HELSINKI
Töölönlahdenkatu 16 C, Helsinki
P.O. Box 38, FI-00097 Uniarts, Finland
+358 40 501 2300, tuomas.auvinen@siba.fi
www.siba.fi, www.uniarts.fi

RSITY
HE ARTS
ELSINKI

× START HERE

UNIVERSITY
THE ART

245

3PM START
MAKERS HALL, CRAFT & CO,
390 SMITH STREET,
COLLINGWOOD VIC 3066
RSVP BY 02 JANUARY 2019
or Die
& ROBBO
2019
TO FOLLOW
Robbo
CRAFT & CO,
STREET,
VIC 3066
JANUARY 2019
INVITE
THEIR
02
ARRIVE

250

SAVE THE DATE
LONG ISLAND
NEW YORK
18.06.21

THE WEDDING OF GILL O'BRIEN & LIAM GRAD

WED
GIL
AI
06.21

ORY, 42-38 9TH ST
NEW YORK, NY

DING
O'BRIEN
GRAD
3PM

NG ISLAND CITY
01

SAVE THE DATE
LONG ISLAND
NEW YORK
18.06.21

THE WEDDING OF GILL O'BRIEN & LIAM GRAD

THE WEDDING
OF GILL O'BRIEN
& LIAM GRA...
18.06.21 - 3PM

THE FOUNDRY, 42-38 9TH ST, LONG
NEW YORK, NY 11101

NEW
YORK
NEW
YO...

NAME(S)

ATTENDANCE   ○YES ○...

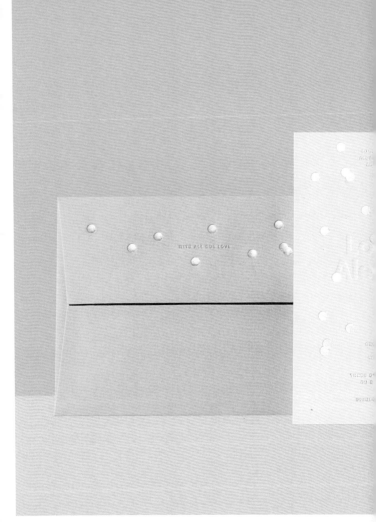

WITH ALL OUR LOVE

257

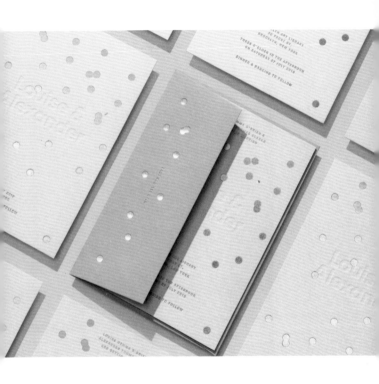

258

Francis
&
James

Francis
&
James

With
all our
love

With
all our
love

266

How to fold this poster:
Sydlexia.org/Learn

Sydlexia

Making
sense of
dyslexia

How to fold this poster:
Sydlexia.org/Learn

Sydlexia

Making
sense of
dyslexia

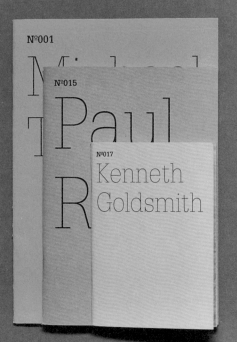

Nº013

G. M.

Nº012

Vandana
Shiva

Nº010

Christoph
Menke

ás

Matthias Sauer
dOCUMENTA 13

Markus Müller
dOCUMENTA (13)

Eva Scharrer
dOCUMENTA [13]

dOCUMENTA (13)

Creative Life
DOCUMENTA (13)

Carolyn Christov-
Bakargiev
dOCUMENTA (13)

dOCUMEN

nd Leifeld
UMENTA (13)

Carolyn Christov–Ba
dOCUMENTA (13)

dOCUMENTA (13)

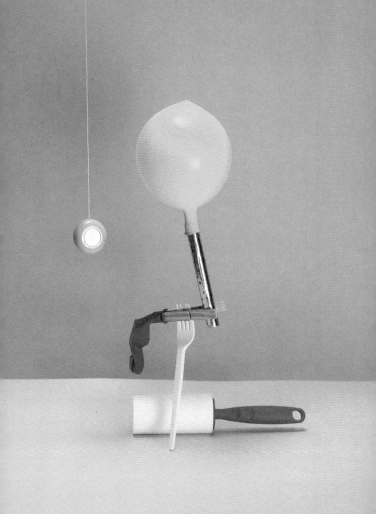

285

"By including the produces' colours and not just their textures, we created a much stronger connection between the original crops and the bowls."

287

Your choice makes
the world better.

ee Beans

ngle Origin

コーヒービーンズ

シングルオリジン

Imperfect Coffee Beans – Carefully selected by buyers from coffee
farmers in Brazil, Guatemala, and around the world, these green
beans have been roasted to the best. Enjoy the coffee's rich,
distinct, and aromatic flavor.

たとえ

取り組

自分た

さい。

Coffee Beans

Signature
Blend

コーヒービーンズ

シグネチャー
ブレンド

What we do may be imperfect,
but let's take a small step together
to make the world and society a better place.

たとえ

取り組

自分た

Imperfect Coffee Beans – Carefully selected by buyers from coffee
farmers in Brazil, Guatemala, and around the world, these green
beans have been roasted to the best. Enjoy the coffee's rich,
distinct, and aromatic flavor.

コーヒーは、ブラジル、グアテマラをはじめ、
世界中のコーヒー農家からバイヤーが吟味して選んだ生豆を、
おいしくなるように焙煎した、個性豊かなコーヒーの風味を、
お楽しみください。

Your choice makes
the world better.

Coffee Beans

Single Origin

コーヒービーンズ

シングルオリジン

Imperfect Coffee Beans --Carefully selected by buyers from coffee farmers in Brazil, Guatemala, and around the world, these green beans have been roasted to the best. Enjoy the coffee's rich, distinct, and aromatic flavor.

コーヒー豆は、ブラジル、グアテマラを筆頭に、各農家から、バイヤーが吟味して選んだ生豆を焙煎した個性豊かなコーヒーの風味をお楽しみください。

What we do may be imperfect, but let's take a small step together to make the world and society a better place.

たとえ

取り組

自分た

Coffee Beans

Signature Blend

コーヒービーンズ

シグネチャー
ブレンド

Imperfect Coffee Beans - Carefully selected by buyers from coffee farmers in Brazil, Guatemala, and around the world, these green beans have been roasted to the best. Enjoy the coffee's rich, distinct, and aromatic flavor.

コーヒー豆は、ブラジル、グアテマラを筆頭に、各農家から、バイヤーが吟味して選んだ生豆を焙煎した個性豊かなコーヒーの風味をお楽しみください。

Your choice mak
the world better

Glazed Nuts

Espresso &
Maple Sugar

Glazed Nuts

Apple &
Chocolate

ard

ソルティ
マスタード

グレーズドナッツ

エスプレッソ
＆
メイプルシュガー

グレーズドナッツ

チョコレート

グレーズドナッツ

www.imperfect-doweli.com

www.imperfect-doweli.com

www.imperfect-d

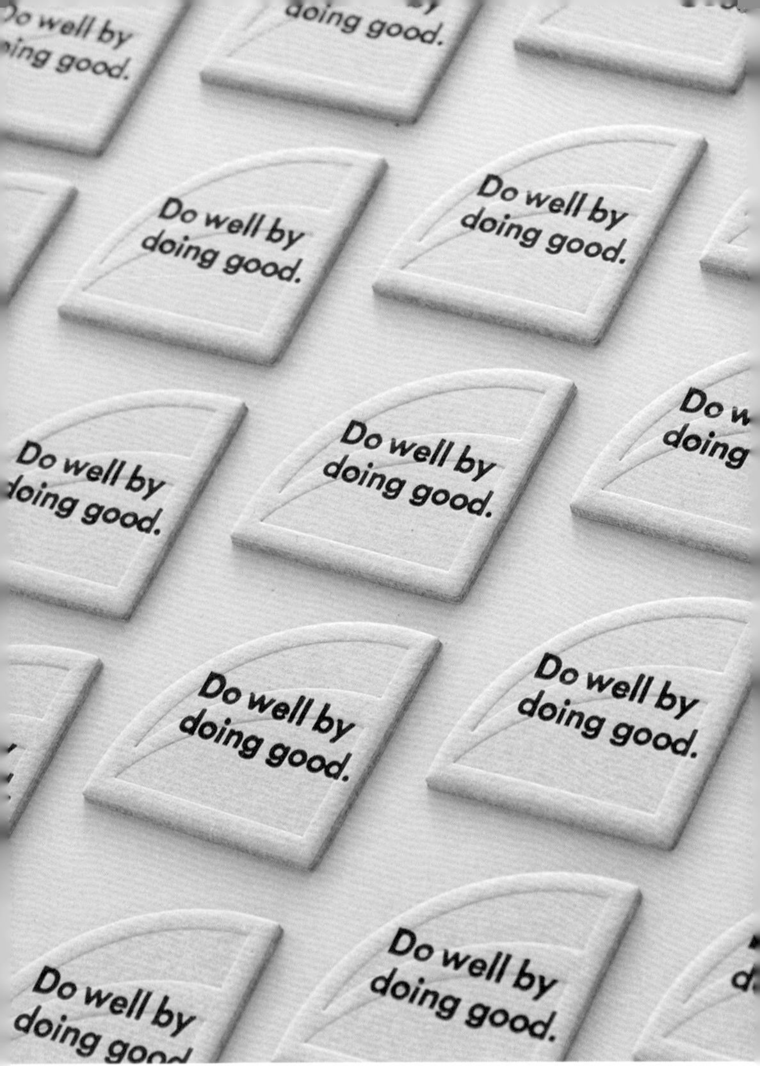
Do well by
doing good.

GIFT BOX

MADE WITH
100% NATURAL INGREDIENTS

BY

Nuagè

Nuagè

CARAMEL WIT

NATURAL INGR
ARTISAN POPCORN

302

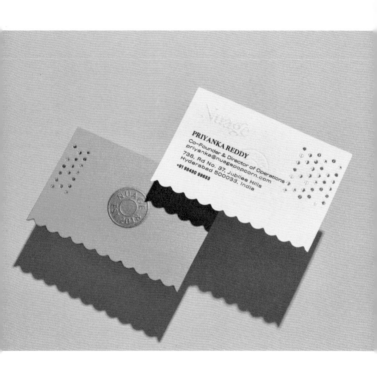

PRIYANKA REDDY
Co-Founder & Director of Operations
priyanka@nuagepopcorn.com
738, Rd No. 37, Jubilee Hills
Hyderabad 500033, India
+91 98490 99623

305

306

SPANISH-STYLE HARD NOUGAT *of* ALICANTE

Made using only the finest ingredients, this product has been handcrafted to create a decadently delicious harmony of flavours, fragrance and textures, authentic to their origins. Naturally free from preservatives, flavours and artificial colours.

NUTRITIONAL INFORMATION

serving size 50g
servings per pack: 3

	per serve	per 100g
Energy	913kj	1826kj
Protein	3.9g	7.7g
Fat - total	8.5g	17.1g
- saturated	1.2g	2.3g
Carbohydrate	31g	62.1g
- sugars	29.2g	58.4g
Sodium	424mg	848mg

Ingredients
Sugar, glucose (from rice), roasted almonds (33%), salt, rosemary honey (5%), vanilla, orange, egg albumen, rice flour, rice paper (potato starch).

MAY CONTAIN TRACES OF OTHER TREE NUTS AND PEANUTS.
Store in a cool, dry place

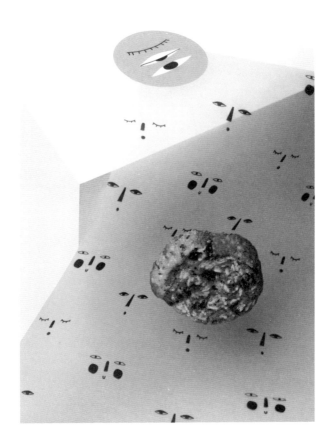

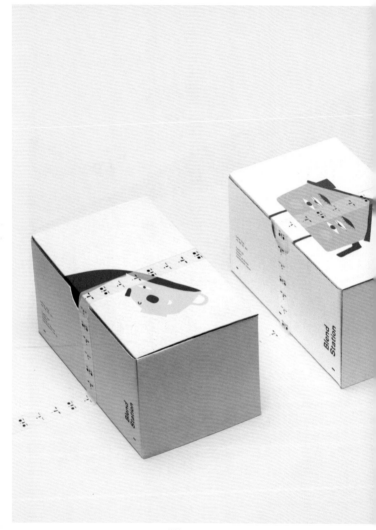

316

317

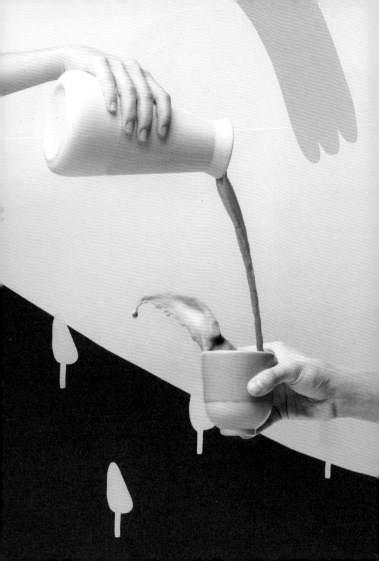

REUSABLE BAMBOO
MAKE-UP REMOVER PADS

ECO AT HEART

14 pack + wash bag
machine washable

324

REUSABLE ORGANIC
COTTON PRODUCE BAGS

ECO AT HEART

~~Tomatoes~~

juice

~~Crackers~~

~~Salsa~~

~~Freezerbags~~

~~Rise~~

~~Cookies~~

~~Eggs~~

Milk

~~Bread~~

~~Cookie~~

"While most packaging takes on bright and aggressive colours, pastel-toned samples often look 'intelligent' and stand out on the shelf."

Soup
Milk
Eggs
Bread

ЯЙЦА
КУРИНЫЕ
ПИЩЕВЫЕ
СТОЛОВЫЕ

6
ШТУК

ОТБОРНАЯ КАТЕГОРИЯ

~~Eggs~~

Milk

~~Bread~~

~~Cookies~~

334

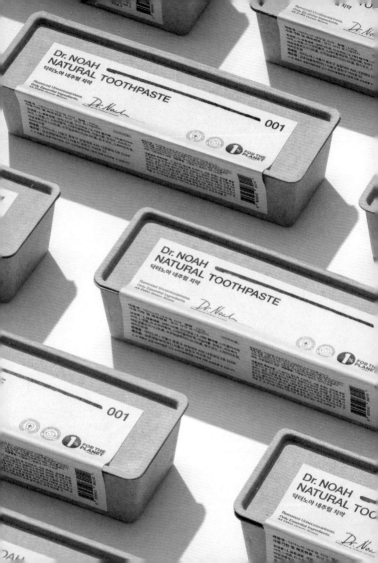

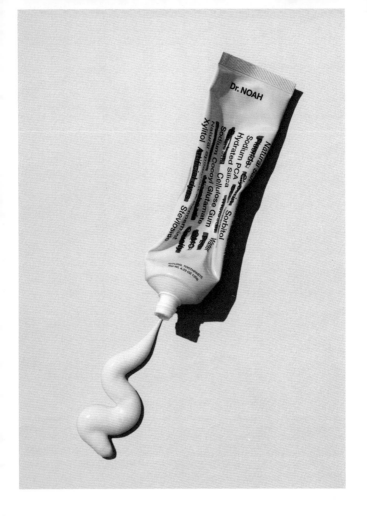

338

Dr. NOAH

PH : neutral, Net Wt. 4.23 OZ (120g)

[✓] All EWG Green Score   [ ] NaF

Dr. Noah Natural Toothpaste (fluoride free)		
Serial no.	001	Safe for Pregnant Women and Babies
	Dr. Noah Natural Toothpaste	1. Only Essential Ingredients
	닥터노아 내추럴 치약	2. All Ingredients : EWG Green Level (Score 1)
E-mail	hello@doctornoah.net	3. Supported by Dr.Noah members
Kakao ID	@drnoah	

Toothpaste Information

닥터노아 내추럴 치약은 임산부와 아기가 사용할 수 있는 안전한 치약입니다

많은 치약들은 인체에 건강을 위협할 수 있는 성분(불소, SLS/SLES, 트리클로산, 미세플라스틱, 인공색소) 등과 화학성분(방부제/부형제)로 치약을 제앙할 때 드는 원료를 비싸면서 더 건강 원료 맞춤 만드는 계면활성제, 감미료(합성감미료) 등을 사용하고 있습니다. 그러나 이러한 물질들은 치약의 상품성을 높여서, 구강건강을 유지하기 위해 꼭 필요한 성분들은 아닙니다. 닥터노아 내추럴 치약에 모든 성분은 EWG 평가 기준 1등급으로 표기된 물질만을 사용하였습니다. 안심하고 사용하셔도 좋습니다.

*EWG: 미국비정부 단체로서 제품의 안전한 치약에 따지는 성분을 연구하는 미국의 비영리 기관입니다.

Ingredients 12가지 전성분	Origin 유래	EWG 등급
001 Natural Salt	Sea 천연 소금	Score 1
002 Sodium Cocoyl Glutamate	Coconut Oil 코코넛오일	Score 1
003 Calcium Carbonate	Calcium Carbonate 탄산칼슘	Score 1
004 Sorbitol	Glucose 식물(옥수수)	Score 1
005 Sodium PCA	Amino Acid 아미노산	Score 1
006 Hydrated Silica	Sand 모래	Score 1
007 Cellulose Gum	Wood 나무	Score 1
008 Xylitol	Xylose 식물(자일로스)	Score 1
009 Stevioside	Stevia 스테비아(식물)	Score 1
010 Natural Spearmint	Spearmint 천연 스피아민트	Score 1
011 Natural Peppermint	Peppermint 페퍼민트	Score 1
012 Water	Water 정제수	Score 1

Not Used Ingredients 닥터노아에서 사용하지 않은 성분들

100 Fluoride	104 Triclosan	108 GMO	112 Artificial dyes
101 Glycerin	105 Microbeads	109 Cruelty	113 Artificial Flavors
102 SLS	106 Mineral Oil	110 PEG	
103 CMIT/MIT	107 Parabens	111 Saccharine	

* More information on the back of this paper. 전성분에 대한 더 많은 정보는 뒷면에 표기되어 있습니다.

RAW INGREDIENTS
REAL FLAVOUR

RAPSCALLION_
SODA®

MADE IN
SCOTLAND

RAW INGREDIENTS
REAL FLAVOUR

S_01
Rhubarb

Sour Face Pull

AVERAGE PER	100 ML
ENERGY (KJ)	84.0 KJ
ENERGY (CAL)	21.0 KCAL
PROTEIN	0.0 G
SATURATED	0.1 G
CARBOHYDRATE	4.9 G
SUGARS	4.9 G
TOTAL FAT	0.2 G
FIBRE	<0.5 G
SODIUM	<0.1 G

INGREDIENTS
CARBONATED WATER,
SCOTTISH RHUBARB,
PINK GRAPEFRUIT
ZEST, SICHUAN PEPPER,
RAW ORGANIC CANE
SUGAR AND VITAMIN C

59 CAL. // @ 250 ML

I'M BEST ENJOYED COLD.
KEEP ME OUT OF DIRECT
SUNLIGHT. ONCE OPENED
DRINK ME IMMEDIATELY.
I'M ALSO VEGAN FRIENDLY.

SCOTTISH RHUBARB,
PINK GRAPEFRUIT ZEST
AND SICHUAN PEPPER

55 CAL. // @ 250 ML

BATCH
19

5 060757 830034

WE'RE RAPSCALLION_SODA.
THE SCOTTISH SOFT DRINK
MANUFACTURERS CRAFTING
SUBVERSIVE SODAS.

WE ALWAYS USE FRESH, RAW
INGREDIENTS. WE NEVER USE
ARTIFICIAL COLOURS, FLAVOURS,
SWEETENERS, PRESERVATIVES
OR CONCENTRATES. THIS IS
OUR PROMISE TO YOU.

RAPSCALLION_SODA
UNIT 10, 30 CUMBERLAND ST,
GLASGOW, SCOTLAND, G3 9DJ
RAPSCALLIONSODA.COM
@RAPSCALLION_SODA

AVERAGE PER	100 ML
ENERGY (KJ)	84.0 KJ
ENERGY (CAL)	21.0 KCAL
PROTEIN	0.0 G
SATURATED	0.1 G
CARBOHYDRATE	4.9 G
SUGARS	4.9 G
TOTAL FAT	0.2 G
FIBRE	<0.5 G
SODIUM	<0.1 G

INGREDIENTS
CARBONATED W
INFUSED WITH
SCOTTISH RHU
PINK GRAPEFRU
ZEST, SICHUAN
RAW ORGANIC
SUGAR AND VI

5 060757 830034

RAW INGREDIENTS
REAL FLAVOUR

RAPSCALLION_
SODA®

MADE IN
SCOTLAND

RAW INGREDIENTS
REAL FLAVOUR

C_03
Dry Lime

Sharp as a Tack

AVERAGE PER	100 ML
ENERGY (KJ)	84.0 KJ
ENERGY (CAL)	21.0 KCAL
PROTEIN	1.0 G
SATURATED	0.0 G
CARBOHYDRATE	2.1 G
SUGARS	2.0 G
TOTAL FAT	0.2 G
FIBRE	0.0 G
SODIUM	<0.1 G

INGREDIENTS
CARBONATED WATER,
FRESH LIME JUICE,
LIME RIND, KAFFIR
LIME LEAF, RAW
ORGANIC CANE SUGAR
AND VITAMIN C

30 CAL. // @ 250 ML

I'M BEST ENJOYED COLD.
KEEP ME OUT OF DIRECT
SUNLIGHT. ONCE OPENED
DRINK ME IMMEDIATELY.
I'M ALSO VEGAN FRIENDLY.

FRESH LIME JUICE,
LIME RIND AND
KAFFIR LIME LEAF

36 CAL. // @ 250 ML

BATCH
23

5 060757 830027

WE'RE RAPSCALLION_SODA.
THE SCOTTISH SOFT DRINK
MANUFACTURERS CRAFTING
SUBVERSIVE SODAS.

WE ALWAYS USE FRESH, RAW
INGREDIENTS. WE NEVER USE
ARTIFICIAL COLOURS, FLAVOURS,
SWEETENERS, PRESERVATIVES
OR CONCENTRATES. THIS IS
OUR PROMISE TO YOU.

RAPSCALLION_SODA
UNIT 10, 30 CUMBERLAND ST,
GLASGOW, SCOTLAND, G3 9DJ
RAPSCALLIONSODA.COM
@RAPSCALLION_SODA

AVERAGE PER	100 ML
ENERGY (KJ)	84.0 KJ
ENERGY (CAL)	21.0 KCAL
PROTEIN	1.0 G
SATURATED	0.0 G
CARBOHYDRATE	2.1 G
SUGARS	2.0 G
TOTAL FAT	0.2 G
FIBRE	0.0 G
SODIUM	<0.1 G

INGREDIENTS
CARBONATED W
FRESH LIME JU
LIME RIND, KA
LIME LEAF, RA
ORGANIC CANE
AND VITAMIN C

30 CAL. // @ 250 ML

I'M BEST EN
KEEP ME OUT
SUNLIGHT. ON
DRINK ME IMM
I'M ALSO VEG

5 060757 830027

RAW INGREDIENTS
REAL FLAVOUR

RAPSCALLION_
SODA®

C_02
Burnt Lemon

Juicy Wee Tart

MADE IN
SCOTLAND

RAW INGREDIENTS
REAL FLAVOUR

AVERAGE PER   100 ML.   INGREDIENTS:

FRESH LEMON JUICE,
CHARRED LEMON ZEST
AND CORIANDER SEED

40 CAL. // 41 250 ML.

BATCH
34

WE'RE RAPSCALLION_SODA
THE SCOTTISH SOFT DRINK
MANUFACTURERS CRAFTING
SURREPTION_SODAS

WE ALWAYS USE FRESH, RAW
INGREDIENTS. WE NEVER USE
ARTIFICIAL COLOURS, FLAVOURS,
SWEETENERS, PRESERVATIVES
OR CONCENTRATES. THIS IS
OUR PROMISE TO YOU.

RAPSCALLION_SODA
RAPSCALLIONSODA.COM
@RAPSCALLION_SODA

5 060757 830010

RAW INGREDIENTS
REAL FLAVOUR

RAPSCALLION_
SODA®

S_03
Cranachan

Sweet Scottish Smooch

MADE IN
SCOTLAND

RAW INGREDIENTS
REAL FLAVOUR

AVERAGE PER   100 ML.   INGREDIENTS:

CARBONATED WATER,
INFUSED WITH
SCOTTISH RASPBERRY,
TOASTED OAT, LEMON
ZEST AND STAR ANISE

10 CAL. // 41 250 ML.

BATCH
52

WE'RE RAPSCALLION_SODA
THE SCOTTISH SOFT DRINK
MANUFACTURERS CRAFTING
SURREPTION_SODAS

WE ALWAYS USE FRESH, RAW
INGREDIENTS. WE NEVER USE
ARTIFICIAL COLOURS, FLAVOURS,
SWEETENERS, PRESERVATIVES
OR CONCENTRATES. THIS IS
OUR PROMISE TO YOU.

RAPSCALLION_SODA
UNIT 10, 30 CUMBERLAND ST,
GLASGOW, SCOTLAND, G5 9QJ
RAPSCALLIONSODA.COM
@RAPSCALLION_SODA

5 060757 830058

RAPSCALLION_
SODA®

C_01
Ginga Ninja

Fiery Throat Kick

COLD PRESSED GINGER,
CASSIA, LEMON ZEST,
CARDAMOM AND PIMENTO

40 CAL. // ℮ 250 ML

RAPSCALLION_
SODA®

C_02
Burnt Lemo

Juicy Wee Tart

FRESH LEMON JUICE,
CHARRED LEMON ZEST
AND CORIANDER SEED

40 CAL. // ℮ 250 ML

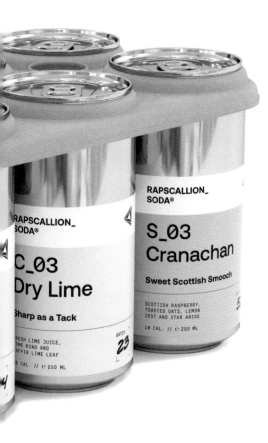

RAPSCALLION_
SODA®

C_03
Dry Lime

Sharp as a Tack

FRESH LIME JUICE,
LIME RIND AND
KAFFIR LIME LEAF

18 CAL. // ⓔ 250 ML

BATCH
23

RAPSCALLION_
SODA®

S_03
Cranachan

Sweet Scottish Smooch

SCOTTISH RASPBERRY,
TOASTED OATS, LEMON
ZEST AND STAR ANISE

18 CAL. // ⓔ 250 ML

346

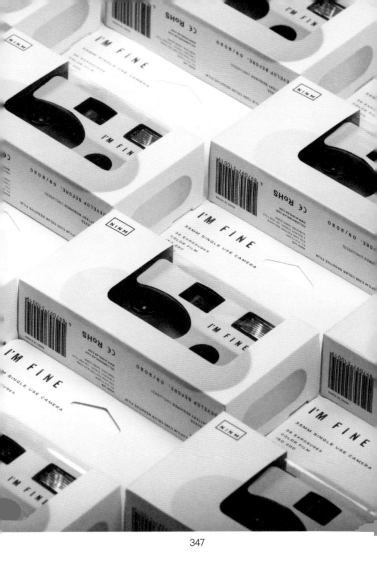

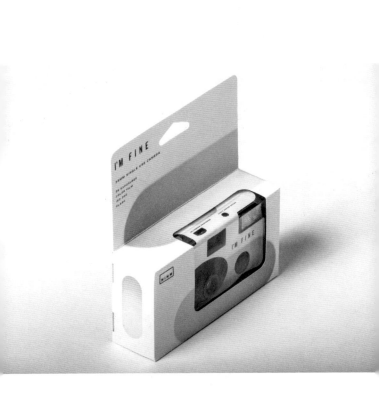

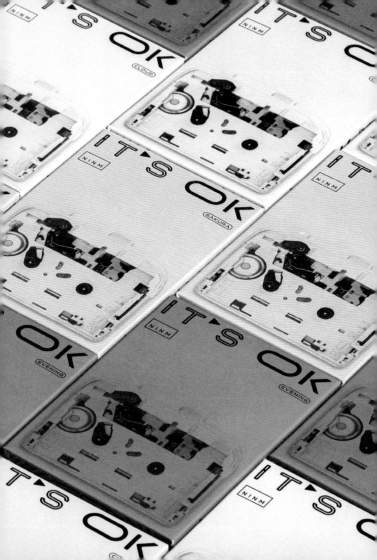

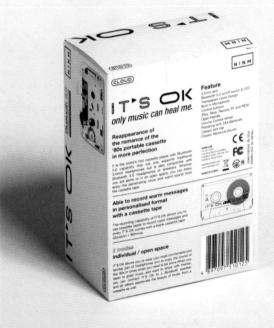

IT'S OK
only music can heal me.

Reappearance of the romance of the '80s portable cassette in more perfection

It is the world's first cassette player with Bluetooth 5.0 capability that not only supports traditional Bluetooth 5.0 headphones but is also compatible with 3.5mm headphones or speakers. Whether you are alone or in an open space, you can freely enjoy the penetrating vocal and warm sound from the cassette tape.

Able to record warm messages in personalised format with a cassette tape

The recording capability of IT'S OK allows you to use cassette tapes to record voice messages and every IT'S OK comes with a blank cassette tape (Duration = 60mins).

2 modes
individual / open space

IT'S OK allows you to wear your most comfortable and familiar pair of headphones and to enjoy the sound of the '90s in times when you need to be busy. When you listen to great music and want to share with friends, you can connect IT'S OK to a Bluetooth speaker and all others appreciate the beauty of music from a cassette as well.

Feature
3.5mm jack
Bluetooth 5.0 on/off switch & LED
Transparent cover Design
Built-in Microphone
Control buttons
(Play, Stop, Record, FF and REW)
Open Handle
Volume Control Wheel
Powering with 2AA Batteries
Cassett belt clip
Classic Monaural Sound

353

354

355

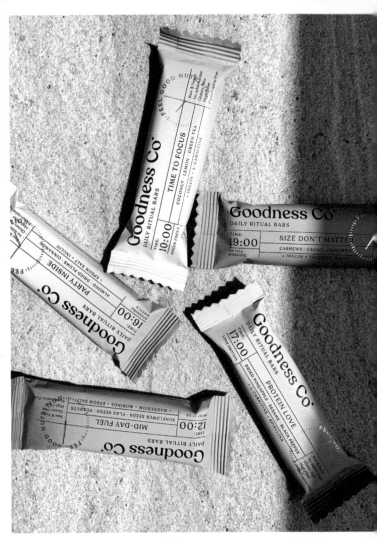

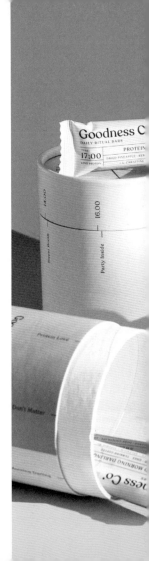

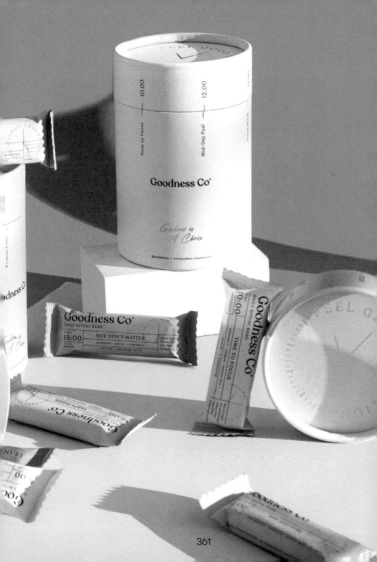

361

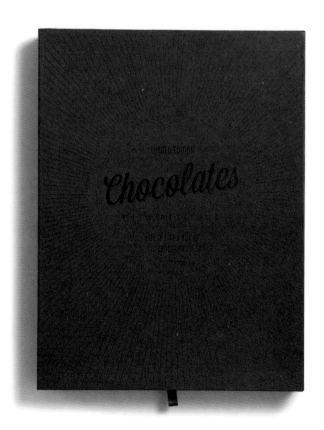

LIMITED EDITION

Chocolates

THE IS LIKE A BOX OF
CHOCOLATES

363

364

Chocolates
~ WITH ATTITUDE ~

THE

Adventurer

LIFE IS EITHER A GREAT
ADVENTURE OR NOTHING

⚓ HELEN KELLER ⚓

— INGREDIENTS —

Take a journey of discovery
with coconut, white chocolate
and exotic fruits.

Chocolates
— WITH ATTITUDE —

THE

CREATOR

IT TAKES A LOT OF HARD WORK
TO MAKE SOMETHING SIMPLE
—
STEVE JOBS

— INGREDIENTS —

Crunchy almond coated
with sweet white chocolate and
sprinkled with a hint of citrus fruit.

369

SURNAM

SURNAME & SURNAME

SURNAME & SURNAME

SURNAME & SURNAME

SURNAME & SURNAME

SURNAME & SURNAME

SURNAME & SURNAME

Lottie Jones
Co-founder
+44 (0)7879 49
lotte@thisissu

6 More Lond
London SE1

+44 (0)2C
thisissurna

CATS & DOGS

377

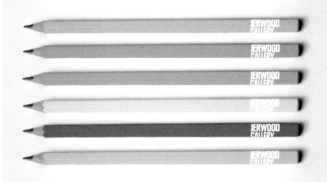

380

Assaggi

BEVANDE FREDDE *(COLD DRINKS)*

San Pellegrino Italienisches Mineralwasser 0,5 / 1	€2.50
San Pellegrino Italienisches Mineralwasser 0,75	€3.50
Acqua Panna stilles italienisches Mineralwasser 0,5 / 1	€2.50
Acqua Panna stilles italienisches Mineralwasser 0,75	€3.50
Coca-Cola 0,3	€2.50
Coca-Cola Light 0,3	€2.50
Fanta 0,3	€2.50
Sprite 0,3	€2.50
Spezi 0,3	€2.50
Schweppes Tonic Water 0,2	€2.50
Schweppes Bitter Lemon 0,2	€2.50
Schweppes Ginger Ale 0,2	€2.50
Mezzomix 0,3	€2.50
Apfelsaft Vollmeyer 0,2	€2.50
Orangensaft Vollmeyer 0,2	€2.50
Tomatensaft Vollmeyer 0,2	€2.50
Kaffeliche Mostgetränke 0,5	€2.50

BEVANDE CALDE *(WARM DRINKS)*

Kaffee Tasse	€2.00
Kaffee	€2.00
Espresso	€2.00
Espresso doppio	€4.00
Latte Macchiato	€2.50
Cappuccino	€3.00
heiße Schokolade	€2.00

382

APERITIVS

ANTIPASTI

PASTA

FROMAGGI

DOLCI

BIRRE

ALCOLICI

LIQUORI & AMARI

VINI DELLA CASA

VINI BIANCHI

VINI ROSSI

385

**ANNE
LESSMEISTER**

×

**ANNE
LESSMEISTER**

×

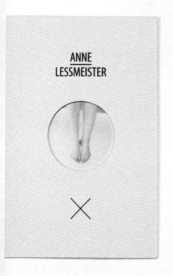

ANNE
LESSMEISTER

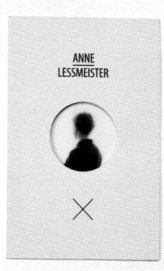

ANNE
LESSMEISTER

390

NORDIC HOUSE

WASHING, DRYING & IRONING

WASHING, DRYING & IRONING

THE

NORDIC HOUSE

SOAP BAR

PEPPERMINT

WASHING, DRYING & IRON

THE

NORDIC HOU

SOAP BAR

BERGAMOT

WASHING, DRYING & IRONING

THE

NORDIC HOUSE

SOAP BAR

WOODS

WASHING, DRYING & IRON

THE

NORDIC HOU

SOAP BAR

FRESH LINE

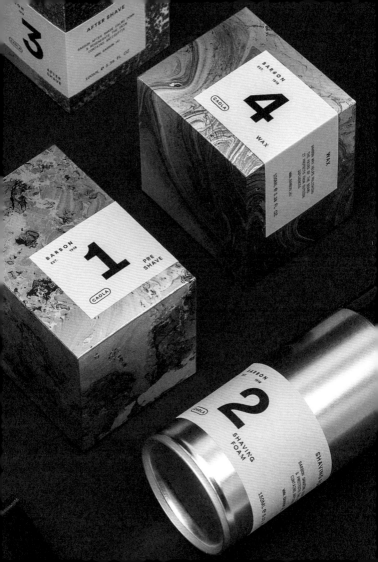

408

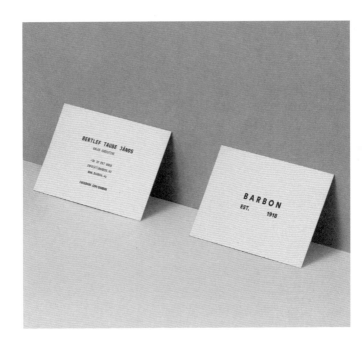

LOEFFLER

OEFFLER RANDALL

F/W 2012 LOOKBOOK
INTRODUCING HANDBAGS

416

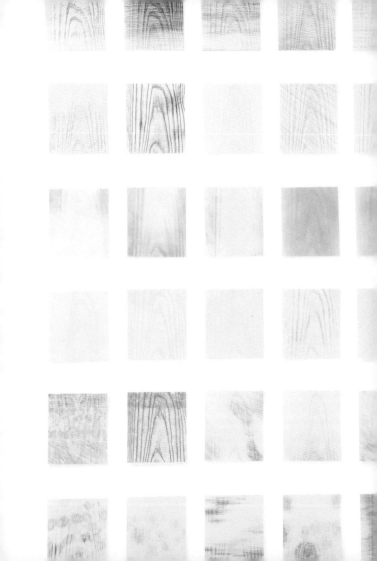

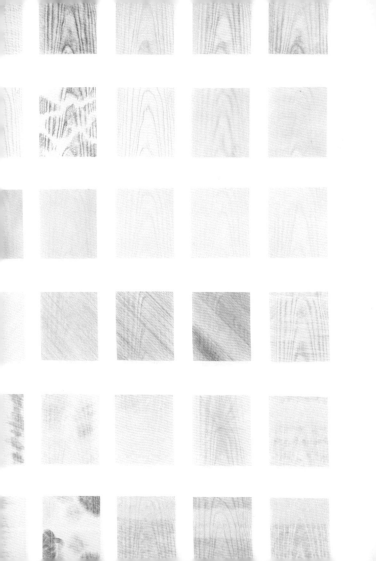

"By manipulating the surfaces, the fusion of subtle shades and raised woodgrains gave us a glimpse into the future of furniture."

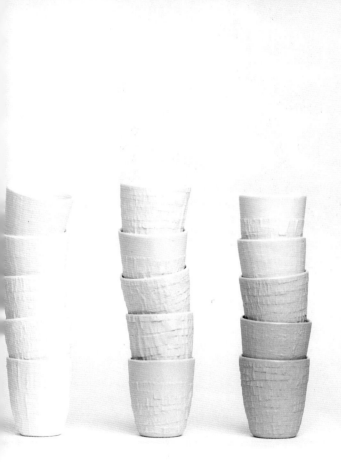

435

Hey

We willen je graag uitnodigen voor onze PALM Hoppluk.

PALM wil zijn liefde voor het ambachtelijke brouwen
met je delen door je in levende lijve te laten zien hoe
PALM Hop Select gebrouwen wordt. Na de geslaagde
hopoogst van vorig jaar word je nu op 1 september
uitgenodigd om te helpen plukken op het eigen hopveld.

Wie graag afsluit met unieke avonturen ontvangen
jou graag om na ho Kasteel Diepensteyn voor een
lekkere bruine, daarna geen wandeling door het eht
de hoppluk Het plukken duurt ongeveer een uurtje
Die dag zijn er trouwens tal van activiteiten gepland
het programma vind je op www.palmhopselect.be!

Bij deze alvast een vooramaakje van ons bier.
Laat ons weten dat je komt op pr@palmbreweries.com
en met hoeveel mensen je komt. Je hoeft uiteraard
niet te plukken - kijken kan ook plezant zijn...

PRAKTISCH
Start – 11u
Einde – 15u

Adres : Kasteel Diepensteyn
Diepensteyn 1, 1840 Steenhuffel.

PALM HOPPLUK

Hey

We willen je graag uitnodigen voor onze PALM Hoppluk.

PALM wil zijn liefde voor het ambachtelijke brouwen met je delen door je in levende lijve te laten zien hoe PALM Hop Select gebrouwen wordt. Na de geslaagde hopoogst van vorig jaar word je nu op 1 september uitgenodigd om te helpen plukken op het eigen hopveld.

Jou wacht absoluut een unieke ervaring! We ontvangen jou graag om 11u op Kasteel Diepensteyn voor een lekkere brunch, de echte start van de hopluk. Het plukken duurt ongeveer een uurtje. Die dag zijn er trouwens nog tal van activiteiten gepland. Het programma vind je op www.palmhopselect.bel

Bij deze alvast een voorsmaakje van ons bier. Laat ons weten als je komt op pr@palmbreweries.com en met hoeveel mensen je komt. Je hoeft uiteraard niet te plukken – kijken kan ook plezant zijn...

PRAKTISCH
Start – 11u
Einde – 15u
Adres – Kasteel Diepensteyn
Diepensteyn 1, 1840 Steenhuffel.

PALM
HOPPLUK

Hey

We willen je graag uitnodigen voor onze PALM Hoppluk.

PALM wil zijn liefde voor het ambachtelijke brouwen met je delen door je in levende lijve te laten zien hoe PALM gebrouwen wordt. Na de geslaagde hopoogst van vorig jaar word je nu op 1 september uitgenodigd om te helpen plukken op het eigen hopveld.

Dat wordt absoluut een unieke ervaring! We ontvangen jou graag om 11u op Kasteel Diepensteyn voor een lekkere brunch, daarna gaan we richting hopveld voor de hoppluk. Het plukken duurt ongeveer een uurtje. Die dag zijn er trouwens tal van activiteiten gepland, het programma vind je op www.palmhopselect.be!

Bij deze alvast een voorsmaakje van ons bier. Laat ons weten als je komt op pr@palmbreweries.com en met hoeveel mensen je komt. Je hoeft uiteraard niet te plukken - kijken kan ook plezant zijn...

PRAKTISCH

Start — 11u
Einde — 15u

Adres : Kasteel Diepensteyn
Diepensteyn 1, 1840 Steenhuffel.

PALM HOPPLUK

Hey

We willen je graag uitnodigen voor onze PALM Hoppluk.

PALM wil zijn liefde voor het ambachtelijke brouwen met je delen door je in levende lijve te laten zien hoe PALM gebrouwen wordt. Na de geslaagde hopoogst van vorig jaar word je nu op 1 september uitgenodigd om te helpen plukken op het eigen hopveld.

Dat wordt absoluut een unieke ervaring! We ontvangen jou graag om 11u op Kasteel Diepensteyn voor een lekkere brunch, daarna gaan we richting hopveld voor de hoppluk. Het plukken duurt ongeveer een uurtje. Die dag zijn er trouwens tal van activiteiten gepland, het programma vind je op www.palmhopselect.be!

Bij deze alvast een voorsmaakje van ons bier. Laat ons weten als je komt op pr@palmbreweries.com en met hoeveel mensen je komt. Je hoeft uiteraard niet te plukken – kijken kan ook plezant zijn...

PRAKTISCH

Start – 11u
Einde – 15u

Adres : Kasteel Diepensteyn
Diepensteyn 1, 1840 Steenhuffel.

PALM HOPPLUK

Hey

We willen je graag uitnodigen voor onze PALM Hoppluk.

PALM wil zijn liefde voor het ambachtelijke brouwen met je delen door je in levende lijve te laten zien hoe PALM gebrouwen wordt. Na de geslaagde hopoogst van vorig jaar word je nu op 1 september uitgenodigd om te helpen plukken op het eigen hopveld.

Dat wordt absoluut een unieke ervaring! We ontvangen jou graag om 11u op Kasteel Diepensteyn voor een lekkere brunch, daarna gaan we richting hopveld voor de hoppluk. Het plukken duurt ongeveer een uurtje. Die dag zijn er trouwens tal van activiteiten gepland, het programma vind je op www.palmhopselect.be!

Bij deze alvast een voorsmaakje van ons bier. Laat ons weten als je komt op pr@palmbreweries.com en met hoeveel mensen je komt. Je hoeft uiteraard niet te plukken – kijken kan ook plezant zijn...

PRAKTISCH

Start – 11u
Einde – 15u

Adres : Kasteel Diepensteyn
Diepensteyn 1, 1840 Steenhuffel.

PALM HOPPLUK

Hey

We willen je graag uitnodigen voor onze PALM Hoppluk.

PALM wil zijn liefde voor het ambachtelijke brouwen met je delen door je in levende lijve te laten zien hoe PALM gebrouwen wordt. Na de geslaagde hopoogst van vorig jaar word je nu op 1 september uitgenodigd om te helpen plukken op het eigen hopveld.

Dat wordt absoluut een unieke ervaring! We ontvangen jou graag om 11u op Kasteel Diepensteyn voor een lekkere brunch, daarna gaan we richting hopveld voor de hoppluk. Het plukken duurt ongeveer een uurtje. Die dag zijn er trouwens tal van activiteiten gepland, het programma vind je op www.palmhopselect.be!

Bij deze alvast een voorsmaakje van ons bier. Laat ons weten als je komt op pr@palmbreweries.com en met hoeveel mensen je komt. Je hoeft uiteraard niet te plukken - kijken kan ook plezant zijn...

PRAKTISCH

Start - 11u
Einde - 15u

Adres : Kasteel Diepensteyn
Diepensteyn 1, 1840 Steenhuffel.

PALM HOPPLUK

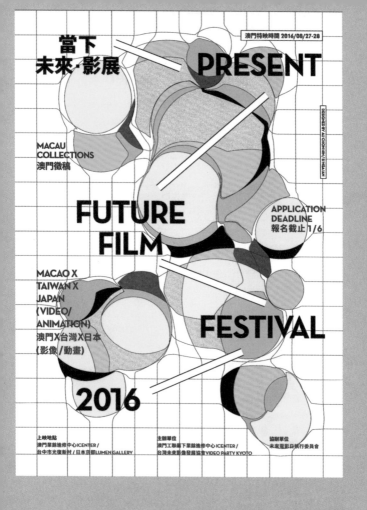

當下
未來・影展

PRESENT

MACAU
COLLECTIONS
澳門徵稿

DESIGNED BY AU CHONHIN / 歐俊軒設計

FUTURE
FILM

APPLICATION
DEADLINE
報名截止 1/6

MACAO X
TAIWAN X
JAPAN
(VIDEO/
ANIMATION)
澳門X台灣X日本
(影像/動畫)

FESTIVAL

2016

上映地點
澳門業餘進修中心ICENTER /
台中市光復新村 / 日本京都LUMEN GALLERY

主辦單位
澳門工聯屬下業餘進修中心 ICENTER /
台灣未來影像發展協會 VIDEO PARTY KYOTO

協辦單位
未來電影日執行委員會

446

當下
未來·影展

澳門特映時間 2016/08/27-28

PRESENT

MACAU
COLLECTIONS
澳門徵稿

FUTURE
FILM

APPLICATION
DEADLINE
報名截止 1/6

MACAO X
TAIWAN X
JAPAN
(VIDEO/
ANIMATION)
澳門X台灣X日本
(影像/動畫)

FESTIVAL

2016

上映地點
澳門美鈺進修中心iCENTER /
台北清光裱新材 / 日本京都LUMEN GALLERY

主辦單位
澳門工創屬下美鈺進修中心iCENTER /
台灣未來影像發展協會VIDEO PARTY KYOTO

協辦單位
未來電影日映行委員會

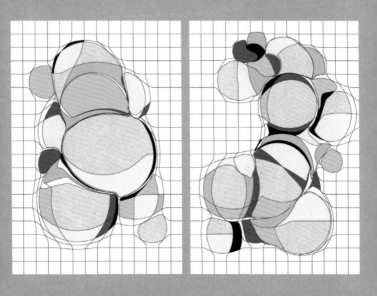

448

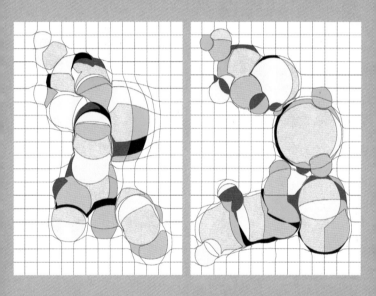

449

WEST
SIDE
STORIES

Ruimte voor de
stadsvernieuwing

Manifestatie
Tentoonstelling
Routes
Lezingen

21.11 – 22.12
2019

www.omirotterdam.nl

WEST
SIDE
STORIES

Ruimte voor
stadsvernieu

LOSE
YOURSELF

**When you become a Member of the V&A,
the world's greatest museum of art and design**

Join today at the Membership Desk,
or at www.vam.ac.uk/membership

GET CLOSER

**When you become a Member of the V&A,
the world's greatest museum of art and design**

Join today at the Membership Desk,
or at www.vam.ac.uk/membership

JOIN US

When you become a Member of the V&A,
the world's greatest museum of art and design

Join today at the Membership Desk,
or at www.vam.ac.uk/membership

JOIN IN

When you become a Member of the V&A,
the world's greatest museum of art and design

Join today at the Membership Desk,
or at www.vam.ac.uk/membership

DIE GROSSE

Kunstausstellung
NRW Düsseldorf 2013

24 / 02
17 / 03

Museum Kunstpalast
www.diegrosse.de

NRW.

DIE GROSSE
Kunstausstellung NRW
Düsseldorf 2013
vom 24. Februar 2013
bis 17. März 2013
Museum Kunstpalast,
Ehrenhof

geöffnet Dienstag
bis Sonntag
von 11 Uhr bis 18 Uhr
Donnerstag und Freitag
11 Uhr bis 21 Uhr

Verein zur Veranstaltung
von Kunstausstellungen e.V.
Telefon 0211/9 10 92 77
von der Ausstellungsvertretung
Büro-Ferien: 0211/492 00 77
www.diegrosse.de
info@diegrosse.de

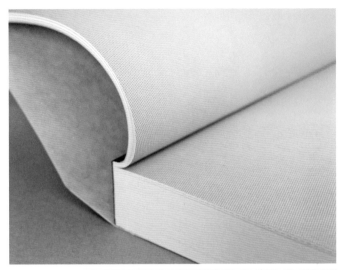

467

BUEN DÍA

Bolivar ønsker å gi deg en følelse av Sør-Amerika –
gjennom maten, vinen, drinkene, musikken og stemningen!
Vår mat er inspirert av retter fra Peru, Brasil, Argentina og Chile.

Lunsj serveres fra kl. 11.00–17.00

BUENAS NOCHES

Bolivar ønsker å gi deg en følelse av Sør-Amerika –
gjennom maten, vinen, drinkene, musikken og stemningen!
Vår mat er inspirert av retter fra Peru, Brasil, Argentina og Chile.
Viva la grill!

BOLÍVAR
Sudamericano bar y brasserie

BUENOS DIAS

Bolivar ønsker å gi deg en følelse av Sør-Amerika –
gjennom maten, vinen, drinkene, musikken og stemningen!
Vår mat er inspirert av retter fra Peru, Brasil, Argentina og Chile.

Brunch serveres fra kl. 12.00-20.00

BOLÍVAR

VINOS POR COPA

Viner på glass   Wines by the glass

Musserende vin

Jaume Serra Cristalino Brut Cava (11 cl)	85,-

Hvitvin

Trapiche Zaphy Chardonnay 2011 (15 cl)	85,-
Trapiche Sauvignon Blanc 2011 (15 cl)	90,-
Viña de los Pajaros Torrontés Palacio Familia Vineyards 2010 (15 cl)	105,-
Nuevas Galerías «Calvinos» Chardonnay 2011 (15 cl)	105,-

Rødvin

Trapiche Zaphy Cabernet Sauvignon 2011 (15 cl)	90,-
Trapiche Cabernet Sauvignon Reserve 2011 (15 cl)	90,-
Leyda «Single Vineyard Los Boludos Pinot Noir 2011 (15 cl)	175,-
Trapiche Malbec «Single Vineyard Vineyard Nevantemix 2007 (15 cl)	400,-

Søtt

Jean Bousquet Malbec Dulce 2009 (6 cl)	75,-
Ketulá Late Harvest Viognier 2008 (6cl)	100,-

SPRING 2013

InWear

LOOKBOOK

INWEAR

Kersti Urvois
President
Casa Decor UK
68 Addison Road
London W14 8JL

T +44 (0)20 7603 8514
F +44 (0)20 7603 8590
M 07793 065949
kurvois@casadecoruk.com
casadecoruk.com

CASA [06]
DECOR

Casa Decor UK
68 Addison Road
London W14 8JL
T + 44 (0)20 7603 8514
F + 44 (0)20 7603 8590
info@casadecoruk.com
casadecoruk.com

CASA [06]
DECOR

Casa Decor UK
68 Addison Road
London W14 8JL
T + 44 (0)20 7603 8514
F + 44 (0)20 7603 8590
info@casadecoruk.com
casadecoruk.com

CASA [06]
DECOR

Casa Decor UK
68 Addison Road
London W14 8JL
T + 44 (0)20 7603 8514
F + 44 (0)20 7603 8590
info@casadecoruk.com
casadecoruk.com

CASA [06]
DECOR

Casa Decor UK
68 Addison Road
London W14 8JL
T + 44 (0)20 7603 8514
F + 44 (0)20 7603 8590
info@casadecoruk.com
casadecoruk.com

Casa Decor (UK) Limited
Registered in England
No 507 4015
Registered Office:
PO Box 896
69-81 Tabernacle Street
London EC2A 4RR

CASA DECOR

Casa Decor UK
68 Addison Road
London W14 8JL
T +44 (0)20 7603 8514
F +44 (0)20 7603 8560
info@casadecor.uk.com
casadecor.uk.com

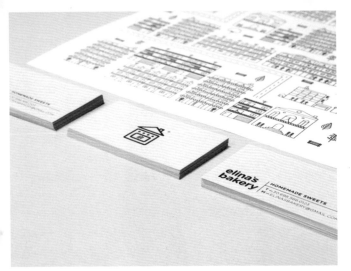

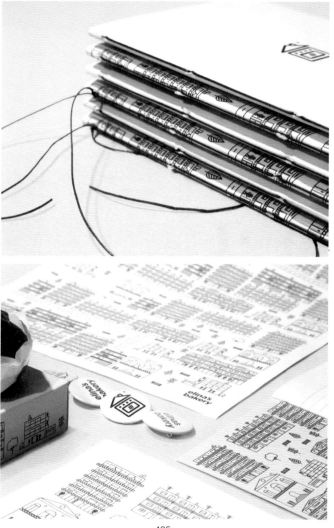

486

487

488

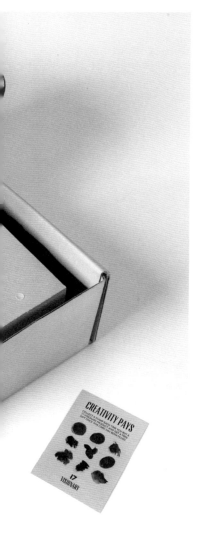

17 VISIONARY

CREATIVITY DELIVERED

491

COME TOGETHER OVER FOOD
This Peace Day, September 21ˢᵗ

Pledge for peace at recipeaceday.org

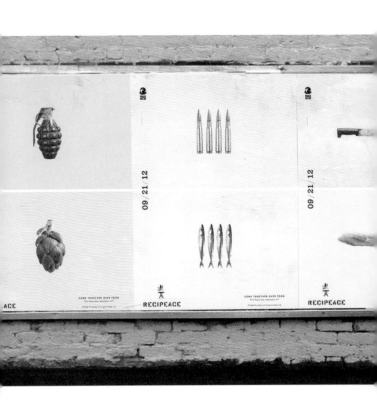

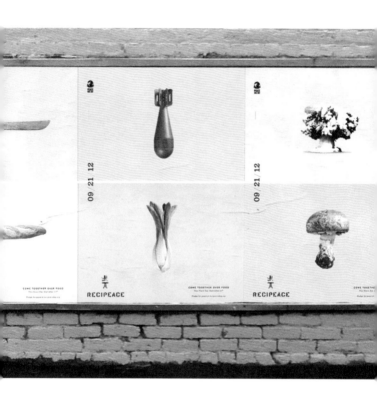

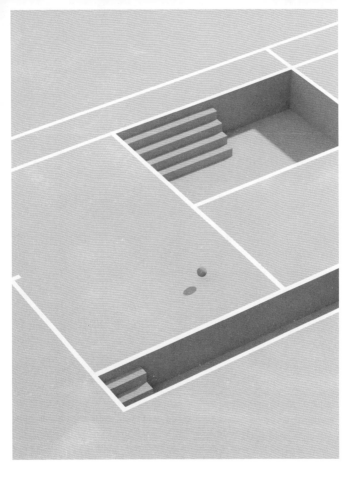

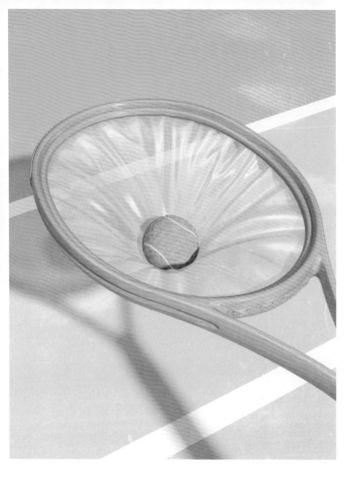

"In fashion, pastels traditionally speak of innocence and femininity; and I enjoy using them in a masculine, industrial way. It's how pastels really come alive for me."

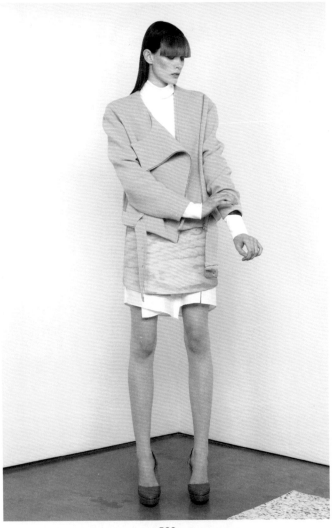

509

515

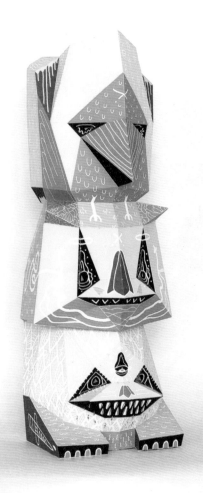

1LB. (500g) NORMAALISUOLAINEN
NORMALSALTAT

Lisäaineeton perinteinen
meijeriovi

LAKTOOSITION

VOI

LACTOSE FREE

Mestres®

COUPAGE

BLUE FIN

— BRUT RESERVA —

マグロに最良のスパークリングワイン

BRUT RESERVA SELECCIONADO POR LOS MEJORES
CHEFS Y SUMILLERS DE BARCELONA Y PARÍS.
RECOMENDADO PARA MARIDAR ESPECIALMENTE
CON ATÚN ROJO SALVAJE.

BRUT RESERVE SELECTED BY THE BEST CHEFS
AND SOMMELIERS FROM BARCELONA AND PARIS.
SPECIALLY RECOMMENDED FOR MARIDAGE
WITH WILD RED TUNA.

— DE LA NOSTRA TERRA A TOT EL MON —

525

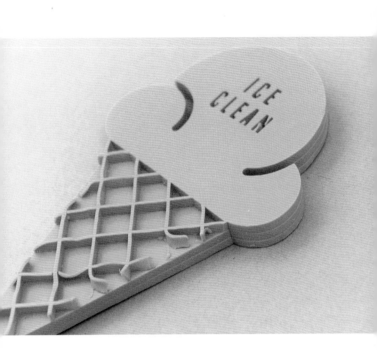

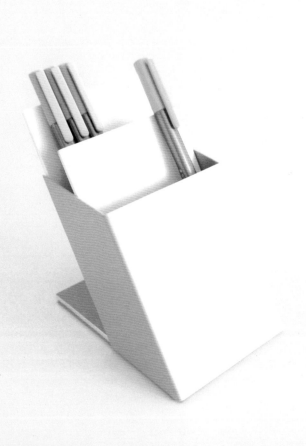

Light,

Bright.

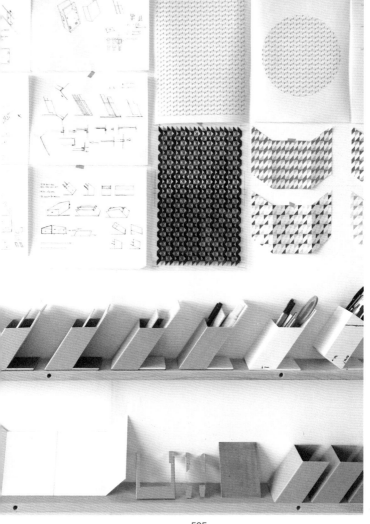

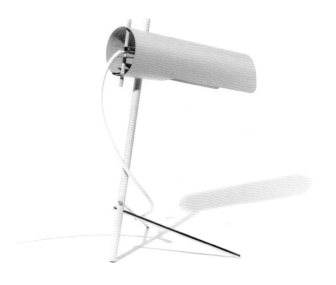

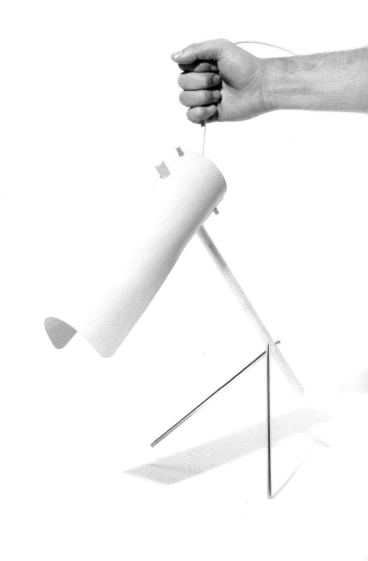

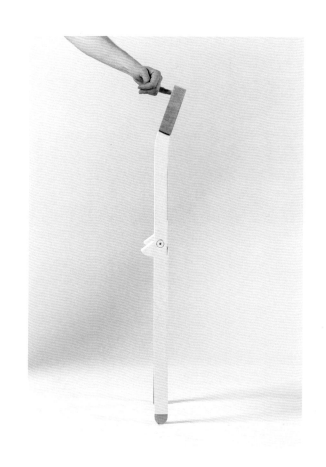

"The colours created in the unique casting process balanced out the asymmetrical forms and gave birth to these objects."

BAR DE PLAYA
. REVOLUCION **40**C,
ITA CP. 63734 MÉXICO
HULASAYULABAR
2   322   139   7049

HULASAYULA.MX

BAR D
AVE. REVO
SAYULITA CP.
@HULAS
2   322

HULASA

PLAYA
JCION **40**C,
3734 MÉXICO
YULABAR
139 7049

ULA.MX

BAR DE PLAYA
AVE. REVOLUCION 4
SAYULITA CP. 63734 M
@HULASAYULABA
52   322 139 70

HULASAYULA.MX

BAR DE PLAYA
AVE. REVOLUCIÓN 40 C
SAYULITA NAYARIT CP. 63734 MÉXICO
@HULASAYULABAR
+52 322 100 7379
+52 329 291 3278

BAR DE PLAYA   AVE. REVOLUCIÓN 40-C
SAYULITA NAYARIT CP. 63734 MÉXICO
@HULASAYULABAR
+52 322 100 7379   +52 329 291 3278

OPEN:
04:00 PM – 5:00 AM

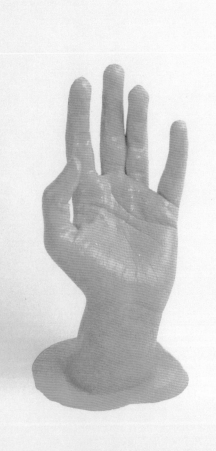

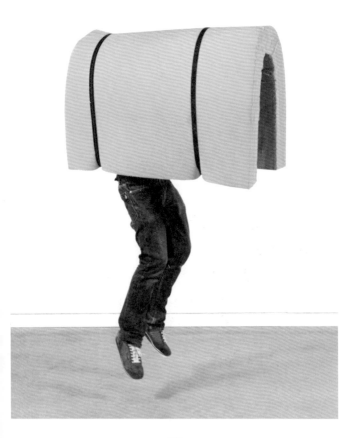

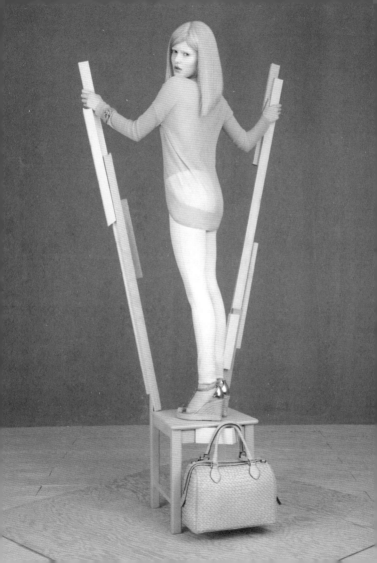

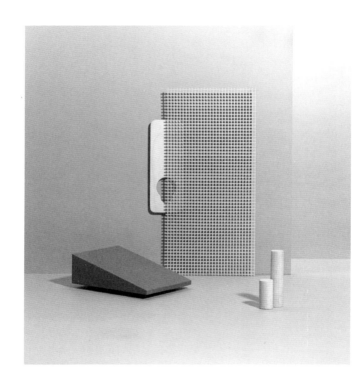

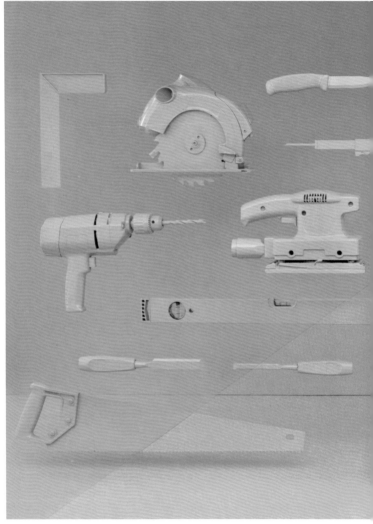

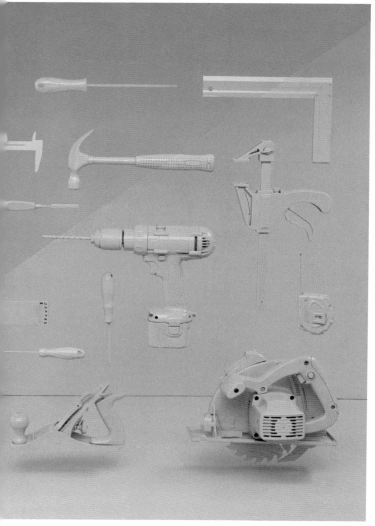

585

"I love the
nostalgic
quality that
[pastels]
provide."

CarteBlanche
/SangJijia

FESTSPILLENE
I BERGEN

GRIEGHALLEN
03. JUNI 2013

DANS
FORESTILLING

OPERA/
MUSIKK

FOR-
BINDEL-
SER

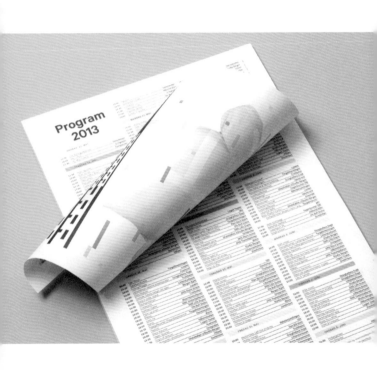

FESTSPILLENE
I BERGEN

SE MER
WWW.FIB.NO

FESTSPILLENE
I BERGEN
2013

Ketil Hvoslef: Samlede kammerverk * Peter Sheppard Skærved * Toke Meldrup * Valdemar Villadsen * Gunnilla Süssman * Tania Tetzlaff
* Herborg Kråkevik * Vilde Frang Bjærke * Christian Ihle Hadland * L'Arpeggiata * The Piazzolla Orchestra * Den skjeggete dame
* Jo Strømgren kompani & Mungo Park * Carte Blanche * Alan Øyen * Tan Dun: Marco Polo * Kristiansand Symfoniorkester
* Susanne Lundeng * Gjertruds sigøynerorkester * Neither med Eir Inderhaug * Tsjekhov: Måken * Music for a While * Den norske solistpris.
* Marius Neset Septet * Håvard Gimse * Trondheimsolistene * Ragnhild Hemsing * Eldbjørg Hemsing * Amalie Skram
* Tore Augestad * Samuel Beckett * Knut Vaage * Elisabeth Holmertz * og mye mer

22. MAI — 05. JUNI
2013

FESTSPILLENE
I BERGEN

SE MER
WWW.FIB.NO

FESTSPILLENE
I BERGEN
2013

Jo Strømgren Kompani & Mungo Park ¤ Cirque Eloize, Cirkopolis ¤ Tan Dun, Marco Polo ¤ Phase 7 ¤ Von Wissen ¤ Camilla Barratt-Due
¤ Lin Rhoden ¤ Music for a While ¤ Marius Neset Septet ¤ Den skjeggete dame ¤ Toro Augustad ¤ Eloge Du Poil ¤ Frode Kvinge Flatland ¤ Jørgen Traren
¤ Stockhaus ¤ Hypertext ¤ Mari Kvien Brunvoll ¤ Empty Bottles Broken Hearts ¤ Ugress ¤ Anna Pettersson ¤ Jeanne Mordoj
¤ Ondt blod ¤ Coelacanth ¤ Desiring Machines ¤ og mye mer

619

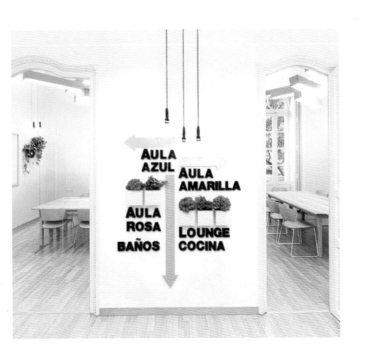

AULA AZUL

AULA AMARILLA

AULA ROSA

LOUNGE COCINA

BAÑOS

INDEX

BIOGRAPHY

100und1

100und1.de

Since 2008, 100und1 has specialised in designing and hand-crafting customised furniture in Berlin. The studio also works on design concepts for homes, retail spaces, gastronomy and the like.

PP. 156-159

6D

6d-k.com

Founded in 2007, 6D is the design office of award-winning art director and graphic designer Shogo Kishino, who works on a wide range of corporate and product branding projects. He also teaches graphic design as an associate professor at Tokyo Ko-gei university.

PP. 290-295

A Black Cover Design

ablackcover.com

A Black Cover Design (ABCD) is a creative studio in Beijing that specialises in branding/visual identities, packaging, UI/UX, and printed matter. Since 2015, its work has been based on a design-driven strategy and systematic communication methodology to serve a variety of clients, winning local and international awards along the way.

PP. 026-031

Alexis Facca

alexisfacca.com

Alexis Facca is a French director, set- and paper designer
based in Brussels who is mainly driven by a passion for
colours, textures, and materials. He creates playful still- and
moving images underlined by bold palettes, smart tricks, and
a handmade tangibility.

PP. 580-583

Alt Group

twitter.com/altgroup

Based in Auckland, Alt Group is an award-winning multi-disciplinary design studio that was founded by Ben Corban and
Dean Poole. Its team members come from diversified back-
grounds in design, business, brand strategy, communication
design, interactive design, and new product development.

PP. 134-139

Ana Mirats Studio

anamirats.com

Based in Barcelona, Ana Mirats Studio works interdisciplin-
arily and through the different areas within design. Its projects stem from a process that is collaborative, dynamic, and
creative, as the team seeks to build organic relationships
with clients big and small.

PP. 080-083, 160-165

Anagrama
anagrama.com

Anagrama is an international design firm with offices in Monterrey and Mexico City, specialising in the design of brands, objects, spaces, software, and multimedia. It thrives on breaking the traditional creative agency scheme, integrating multi-disciplinary teams of creative and business experts.

PP. 188-191, 206-213, 296-305, 394-397

ANTI
anti.as

ANTI is a multi-disciplinary agency in Norway that believes in the potential of the unexpected, the power of interference, and that diversity generates the most impactful ideas. From the intersection of creativity, business, culture, and technology, it leads brands into creating cultural conversations.

PP. 610-617

Áron Filkey
aronfilkey.com

Áron Filkey is a designer and art director who develops unique visuals for commercials, TV shows, art events, music videos, and more. His skills include directing, photography, motion design, graphic design, production design, set/prop design, and photo illustration.

PP. 278-283

artless Inc.

artless.co.jp

artless Inc. is an independent global branding agency with offices in Tokyo, Osaka and Kyoto. Instead of differentiating between art, design, architecture, digital, and other mediums, it embraces the diverse challenges that extend across multiple disciplines. Rooted in Japanese aesthetics, its philosophy is infused with contemporary creativity.

PP. 434-437

Astrid Ortiz

astridortiz.com

Astrid Ortiz is an independent graphic designer based in Barcelona who specialises in visual identities, editorial design, and web design. She brings concepts to life through typography, colours, and shapes customised for each client to ensure lasting outcomes.

PP. 010-013

Atipus

atipus.com

Atipus is an award-winning Barcelona-based graphic design studio that was founded in 1998. The team believes in doing conceptual, creative, and simple work across a variety of media and fields, ranging from branding and packaging to web services.

PP. 018-021, 170-175

Bessermachen DesignStudio

bessermachen.com

At the heart of Bessermachen in Copenhagen lies a passion for design. Instead of merely creating new looks or forms, the studio believes that its work should be a direct, all-compassing reflection of a client, product or organisation. Partnering with those who dare to push the bar further, it specialises in branding and packaging, underlined by strong ideas.

PP. 362-367

Bielke&Yang

bielkeyang.com

Founded in 2012, Bielke&Yang is a studio that specialises in branding and identity design. Working with a diverse selection of clients, from small start-ups to established companies and organisations, it delivers bespoke solutions rooted in usability, creativity, aesthetics and craft.

PP. 176-181

Blok Design

blokdesign.com

Blok Design collaborates with thinkers and creators from all over the world on projects that blend cultural awareness, a love of art, and a belief in humanity to advance society and business alike. It works across media and a variety of disciplines with a ferocious passion.

PP. 120-123, 198-205

BOICUT

boicut.com

Austrian artist BOICUT's work is for the most part illustrative, combining impulsive lines and shapes. His work is inspired by pop culture, skateboarding, the beauty of mundane objects, and urban environments.

PP. 512-517

BOND Creative Agency

bond-agency.com

Bond is an internationally awarded brand and experience design agency comprising a versatile and collaborative team of designers, technologists, and storytellers working globally across its studios in Helsinki, London, San Francisco, Dubai, and Tallinn. True to its Nordic roots, its work is defined by the belief that in an ever-more complex world, simple wins.

PP. 240-243

BOWYER

bowyer.kr

BOWYER is a design studio based in Seoul. Founded in 2016 by Hwayoung Lee and SangJoon Hwang, it specialises in brand identities, print, and exhibitions for a variety of clients.

PP. 214-221

Bunch

Bunch was a leading creative studio offering a diverse range of work spanning branding, literature, as well as digital- and motion design. Established in 2002 with an international reach, it had an in-house team of specialists to deliver intelligent and innovative cross-platform solutions in communication design.

PP. 032-039

Claire Hartley

clairehartley.com

As a freelance graphic designer/studio, Claire Hartley enjoys working with independent brands and thrives on speaking directly with the founders to support them along every step of their journey. She specialises in brand identities, print, and packaging, taking on projects that she genuinely connects with to grow brands through beautiful and meaningful design.

PP. 324-329

---

clase bcn

clasebcn.com

clase bcn is a design and communication studio in Barcelona that specialises in identities and creative direction in fashion, furniture design, art, gastronomy, and more. It seeks to create a unique voice in adding value to brands through conceptually- and visually rich solutions.

PP. 040-041, 523-525

Daniel Ting-Chong

danieltingchong.com

Daniel Ting-Chong is a designer and illustrator based in Cape Town who has been featured in various notable publications including Los Logos, Communication Arts, Fast Company, Computer Arts Projects, and Photoshop Advanced. Born in 1987, he works on a variety of commissions from high-profile clients and collaborators.

PP. 526-529

Depot WPF

depotwpf.com

Depot is an award-winning branding agency in Russia that seeks to bring happiness to its clients. Besides creating brands from scratch and renewing existing ones, it also conducts market analyses, develops strategies, and designs packaging in building integrated communications systems.

PP. 330-333, 518-521

Edith Rose Studio

edithrose.com.au

Edith Rose Studio was born out of the desire to bring a high fashion aesthetic to the world of wedding and event stationery. Their work focuses on the development of distinctive, thoughtful design solutions that capture the individual personalities of each client. Skilfully handcrafted, all pieces are created using traditional letterpress and hot foil printing techniques.

PP. 248-263

Eila Llarena Aliaño

eylallarena.com

Eila Llarena Aliaño is a 2D/3D graphic designer with a not-so-secret love for colours, shapes, and the '80s.

PP. 368-371

Foreign Policy Design Group

foreignpolicy.design

Foreign Policy in Singapore is an award-winning design bureau and think tank of artists, scientists, problem-solvers, polymaths, storytellers, and strategists translating today's ideas into tomorrow's experiences.

PP. 062-067, 244-247

Freytag Anderson

freytaganderson.com

Freytag Anderson is an award-winning creative studio that helps businesses communicate using simple, powerful ideas. From its offices in Glasgow and Oban, the team designs and develops logos, identity systems, brochures, packaging, websites, apps, and everything else in between.

PP. 340-345

Futura

byfutura.com

Futura is a creative studio based in Mexico City, founded with the goal of transforming the way design is developed and consumed globally. Its work is the result of constant experimentation that places creativity above all else, translated into images, objects, and spaces.

PP. 182-187, 314-323, 398-403, 548-557

Greige.

greige.de

Greige. is the creative practice of Mark Kiessling and Birthe Haas in Berlin that runs on a hands-on approach and an open mind. Originally founded as an interdisciplinary design studio in 2001 with team members and international clientele, its scope of work was eventually streamlined to elaborate print projects and book design.

PP. 050-053

Grid London

gridlondon.com

Grid London is the creative studio of independent designer Ashwin Patel. Working with both agencies and private clients, his repertoire spans across branding/identities, print- and digital design, typography, and illustration in the property, financial, technological, social, educational, and retail sectors.

PP. 152-155

groovisions
groovisions.com

Originally formed in Kyoto in 1993, goovisions is a design studio based in Tokyo that primarily focuses on graphics and video work. Its portfolio spans a variety of fields including music, product design, interiors, fashion, and the web.

PP. 054-061, 076-077

HEISME studio

HEISME was an independent creative studio that worked in the space where craft, design, and technology converge. It produced graphic identities, detailed print work, exceptional digital designs, innovative web solutions, and custom video productions. The studio merged with Supermachine in 2014.

PP. 438-445

Heydays
heydays.no

Heydays is an Oslo-based design studio that creates strong visual concepts to trigger curiosity, create excitement and show ambition. They listen, research, and challenge; removing noise to add value.

PP. 088-093, 468-471

Homework / Jack Dahl

homework.dk

A creative agency and design consultancy founded by Jack
Dahl, Copenhagen-based Homework specialises in brand
expressions, visual identities, and packaging within the luxury
and lifestyle industries. Once an art director for international
men's fashion magazines, Dahl has also worked with the
world's most prestigious style, beauty, and luxury brands.

PP. 472-477

Huang Hsin-Chun

Huang Hsin-Chun studied commercial design at the Chung
Yuan Christian University, graduating in 2011. He has won the
EPSON Creative Design Competition, Gold Butterfly Award,
and New Generation Book Cover Design Competition.

PP. 084-087

Impact BBDO

impactbbdo.com

Part of the global BBDO network, IMPACT BBDO is a leading
communications group operating across the Middle East
and North Africa. It was established in the region in 1971 by
Alain Khouri.

PP. 264-269

Jenny van Sommers

jennyvansommers.com

Jenny van Sommers lives and works in London. Her editorial clients include AnOther Magazine and Vogue; while her advertising clients include Apple, Audi, Hermes, and Nike. She counts George Condo, Kurt Schwitters, and Sarah Lucas among her inspirational influences.

PP. 140-143

Joy Li

joyli.com.au

Joy is a graphic designer and illustrator based in Sydney. Her work examines the intersection where design meets gender, race, and cultural studies.

PP. 306-309

Kent Miller

7d8.co

Kent Miller is a co-founder of 7D8, an independent art and design studio. Always open to new ideas and challenges, its multi-disciplinary portfolio reflects the team's flexibility and enthusiasm for collaborations. Through thoughtful research and exploration, it utilises design to create clear messages.

PP. 074-075

Keri Thornton

With a passion and admiration for exceptional design, concepts, and craftsmanship, Keri Thornton creates quality footwear and accessories with thought and personality. She is equally appreciative of the aesthetically bold and bright, as she is of the simple and sophisticated.

PP. 486-491

Knauf and Brown

Knauf and Brown was founded by Calen Knauf and Conrad Brown in Vancouver. Driven by an unnatural obsession with studying spaces and objects, they infused strong aesthetic experiences from their own image-based practices (in particular, Calen's graphic design background and Conrad's one in photography) into their collaborative work.

PP. 538-541

Leftloft
leftloft.com

Leftloft is an independent graphic design company with offices in Milan and New York, and a co-founder of the Ministero della Grafica, a cultural association promoting design culture. Its partners teach design at the Politecnico University of Milan and IUAV Venice.

PP. 270-277

Leo Burnett Chicago

leoburnett.com

The design department of Leo Burnett Chicago operates like a small design studio, comprising smaller design groups that focus on specific clients and opportunities. It strives to collaborate internally and with clients to create purposeful design within advertising. Its work has been awarded locally and internationally.

PP. 492-495

Liquan Liew

rippleroot.com

Liquan Liew grew up in Malaysia, graduated from Melbourne, and is currently based in Singapore. His work is commissioned by a diverse group of clients spanning the arts, culture, hospitality, and commerce. He enjoys mixing graphic design and illustration on print, visual identities, and image-making projects.

PP. 128-133

Liz Wilson

Liz Wilson is a fashion designer from New Zealand who founded the womenswear label, EUGÉNIE.

PP. 506-511

Lotta Nieminen

lottanieminen.com

Lotta Nieminen Studio creates holistic design solutions across disciplines. Passionate about finding the best tools to execute content-driven visuals, it works as a creative partner in all aspects branding, bringing identities to life through thoughtfully crafted print- and digital implementations.

PP. 014-017

magma design studio

magmadesignstudio.de

magma is a graphic design studio focusing on visual appearances, publications, and typography. It develops appropriate and specific communication solutions in a dialogue with clients based on the respective requirements, content, contexts, and a contemporary visual culture.

PP. 166-169

Masquespacio

masquespacio.com

Masquespacio is an award-winning creative consultancy founded by Ana Milena Hernández Palacios and Christophe Penasse. Combining interior design and marketing, it customioes branding and interior solutions through a unique approach that results in fresh and innovative concepts for clients across the world.

PP. 622-624

Mildred & Duck

mildredandduck.com

Mildred & Duck is a Melbourne-based graphic design and communication studio established by Sigiriya Brown and Daniel Smith. It designs for print-, digital-, and environmental media across a variety of sectors in creating thoughtfully crafted outcomes that communicate and connect with people.

PP. 094-097

mischer'traxler

mischertraxler.com

Balancing craftsmanship and technology, Vienna-based mischer'traxler envisions whole systems, new production methods and kinetic/interactive installations that question topics, tell stories or open up new ways of doing things.

PP. 284-289

molistudio

molistudio.com

molistudio is a 3D art direction and design boutique based in Buenos Aires. Founded by sensible, passionate storytellers with a whimsical take on the everyday, its award-winning team is consistently on the lookout for a deep sense of colour and a strong use of metaphors.

PP. 496-505

Morphoria Design Collective

morphoria.com

The Morphoria Design Collective is an award-winning communication design studio based in Düsseldorf that focuses on a conceptual approach underlined by the highest design standards, regardless of the medium.

PP. 462-467

mostlikely

mostlikely.at

mostlikely studio combines architecture, computer graphics, and design in projects that vary from buildings and art installations to videos to product design.

PP. 512-517

NB

nbstudio.co.uk

The award-winning NB designs brands in London. Owned and run by creative directors Nick Finney and Alan Dye, the studio believes in simplicity, empathy, and impact through design. It also seeks big challenges from brave organisations looking for bold solutions and measurable results in delivering strategic creativity across digital and traditional channels.

PP. 372-375, 478-481

nendo
nendo.jp

Founded by architect Oki Sato in 2002, nendo in Tokyo sets out to bring small surprises to people through multi-disciplinary practices of different media including architecture, interiors, furniture, industrial products, and graphic design.

PP. 418-427

Officefordesign

Officefordesign was founded as the collaborative practice of Mirko Spaccapanico and Andrea Palmioli. An interior- and industrial designer, Mirko constantly experiments on materials, whereas architect, designer, and urban planner Andrea is fascinated by urbanisation in Asia.

PP. 618-621

Peltan-Brosz Studio
peltan-brosz.com

Since 2011, Peltan-Brosz Studio has been helping brands, individuals, and institutions express their vision by offering straight-forward creative services. The team is passionate and always on the lookout for meaningful perspectives to add value to the work it does.

PP. 404-409

perezramerstorfer design & creative studio

perezramerstorfer.com

An Austro-Spanish multi-disciplinary studio with a focus and passion for visual identities, perezramerstorfer design & creative studio helps brands, institutions, events, and companies on projects ranging from small initiatives to global campaigns. It believes in creating unique, consistent, and coherent work.

PP. 386-393

Peter Lundstrom Photography

peterlundstrom.com

Peter Lundstrom is a Swedish photographer and art director who works across a broad spectrum of branding and advertising projects.

PP. 584-585

Power-nap Over Design Studio

powernapover.com

Power-nap Over is a Hong Kong-based design studio that was founded in 2013 by Vita Mak who completed his Bachelor of Graphic Design at RMIT University. Vita believes that design can be a tool of social change or at the very least, a means to influence people to live well.

PP. 346-355

Raw Color

rawcolor.nl

Raw Color materialises colour by blending design disciplines
that include graphics, photography, and product design.
From their Eindhoven-based studio, co-founders Daniera ter
Haar and Christoph Brach work together with their team on
self-initiated and commissioned projects.

PP. 022-025, 567-573

RoAndCo

roandcostudio.com

RoAndCo is an award-winning creative studio bringing
thought, relevance, and style to forward-thinking fashion,
beauty, tech, and lifestyle brands. Founded in 2006 by
Roanne Adams, it works intuitively to pinpoint the most
essential, visceral quality with which to tell a brand's story –
aligning inspiration with business objectives.

PP. 410-417

Rose

rosedesign.co.uk

Rose specialises in creating, evolving, and developing
world-class brands. As part of the DIT Creative Taskforce
comprising the UK government's top creative agencies for
exporting the best of British design around the world, the
award-winning studio helps clients connect more success-
fully with its audiences.

PP. 376-379, 458-461

Samuel Henne

samuelhenne.com

Artist and photographer Samuel Henne studied fine arts and communication design at the Braunschweig University of Art. His work has been exhibited widely in Germany as well as galleries and museums worldwide.

Scholten & Baijings

Scholten & Baijings was the Amsterdam-based collaborative practice of Stefan Scholten and Carole Baijings, who have parted ways to pursue individual creative challenges. As a graduate of the Eindhoven Design Academy and a self-taught designer respectively, the pair's award-winning work continues to sell and be exhibited all over the world.

Studio Born

studioborn.co

Studio Born is an independent design studio specialising in branding, packaging and graphic design. Founded by Ebru Sile Göksel and Ipek Eriş Uğurlu who joined forces in early 2017, its passion lies in transforming good ideas into good design and making brands into natural-born storytellers.

Studio Hausherr

Studio Hausherr was a graphic design agency based in Berlin that specialised in corporate, editorial and web design for clients in the field of art, fashion, and culture. As of 2016, it became part of Cee Cee Creative, a multi-disciplinary agency focusing on consulting, design, content, and events.

PP. 380-385

Studio Ongarato
studioongarato.com.au

Under its co-founder and creative director Fabio Ongarato's leadership, Studio Ongarato has garnered global recognition for design excellence over the years. One of Australia's pre-eminent creatives, Ongarato's carefully considered, highly creative process champions unique brand cultures, which he believes should form the basis of individual narratives.

PP. 042-049

Studio PS
studio-ps.nl

Studio PS is a Dutch design studio exploring tactility, refinement, and simplicity through craftsmanship. Its portfolio comprises original products and interiors that are functional in form and tactile in use. With a strong dedication to quality, its work is based on a constant dialogue.

PP. 428-433

Studio Spass

studiospass.com

Studio Spass is a Rotterdam-based agency that works across print, branding, web and spatial design projects as well as animation and photography. Founded by Jaron Korvinus and Daan Mens in 2008, the studio combines a rigorous, considered, and intelligent approach with a playful sensibility.

PP. 450-457

---

studiowmw

studiowmw.com

Based in Hong Kong but working in the global marketplace, studiowmw is a new kind of design agency that specialises in brand-building through effective, captivating and conceptual design solutions. The agency develops trusted relationships with clients to deliver value through visual identities, packaging products, interior- and web design.

PP. 222-229

Svenja Eisenbraun

svenjaeisenbraun.de

Svenja Eisenbraun is a designer in Cologne who loves beautiful paper, typography, and sneakers. In addition to freelance projects, she also works with FOND OF's in-house agency for commercial clients.

PP. 116-119

SWNA
theswna.com

Established in 2009 by Sukwoo Lee, SWNA is a design office located in the highly inspirational city of Seoul. The team comprises a group of passionate designers who experiment with design processes and cross over different fields to create a meaningful world.

PP. 334-339

Sylwana Zybura
sylwanazybura.com

Sylwana Zybura is a fine art and fashion photographer, character designer, and creative director. She is known for her distinctive style that combines high fashion elements with abstract and conceptual ideas, focusing on textures, patterns, and the interconnection of the sculptural human body, art, and design.

PP. 574-579

Terrible Twins
terribletwins.se

Based in the heart of the Swedish countryside in the scenic county of Dalarna, Terrible Twins was founded in 2006 by sisters, designers, and product developers Sara and Karin Ström. Honesty and a natural simplicity are at the heart of the business, along with a strong focus on sustainable local production, environmental awareness, and social engagement.

PP. 586-595

The Birthdays™

thebirthdaysdesign.com

The Birthdays in Athens was founded by Konstantina Yianna-kopoulou and George Strouzas in 2013. The design studio's approach is underlined by a strong focus on typographic systems across a wide range of applications and media. Besides being published by international magazines, its work has also been awarded in local and global competitions.

PP. 482-485

THINGSIDID

behance.net/thingsidid

THINGSIDID is a Hong Kong-based creative studio that is committed to branding, print, graphics, and packaging for clients in the corporate, retail, art and cultural sectors. It seeks to create work that leaves lasting impressions and brings people together.

PP. 104-107

Torafu Architects

torafu.com

Founded in 2004 by Koichi Suzuno and Shinya Kamuro, Torafu Architects works on a diverse range of projects that span architectural design, interior design, product design, spatial installations, and filmmaking. Based in Tokyo, the team has received multiple awards including the Design for Asia (DFA) Grand Award and the Elita Design Awards Grand Prize.

PP. 098-103

UNTITLED MACAO

untitledmacao.com

UNTITLED MACAO is an award-winning design company
that was founded by two young and enthusiastic designers.
Its work encompasses branding, wayfinding, website- and
signage design for clients from all over the world.

PP. 230-239, 446-449

Veronika Levitskaya

behance.net/nikalevitskaya

Veronika Levitskaya is a graphic designer from Russia who
specialises in creating brand identities.

PP. 108-115

Vicente García Morillo

vicentemorillo.com

Vicente García Morillo is a creative director, graphic designer, and illustrator whose work spans across advertising,
fashion, editorial design, and digital experiences. Besides
setting up his own practice, he also co-founded multi-disciplinary design studio Burn & Broad and the 'Made by We Are'
project with former Nike art director Eugene Serebrennikov.

PP. 068-073

Violaine & Jérémy

violaineetjeremy.fr

Founded by Jérémy Schneider and Violaine Orsoni, Violaine & Jérémy is a multi-disciplinary creative studio in Paris focusing on graphic design, typography, and illustration. Dedicated to delivering beautiful messages, it believes in beauty, refinement, delicacy, and timelessness.

PP. 124-127

WAAITT™

waaitt.dk

WAAITT is a non-award-winning creative agency that develops bespoke visual- and auditory design solutions for pleasant people. Its approach is manifested in its full name: 'We Are All In This Together'. Centrally located in Copenhagen, the studio was established by graphic designers Anders Rimhoff, Jess Jensen and Dennis Müller in the summer of 2011.

PP. 192-197

Wang Zhi-Hong Studio

wangzhihong.com

Wang Zhi-Hong is a leading graphic designer in Taiwan. An AGI member, he has received numerous international accolades, including Kasai Kaoru's Choice Award at the HKDA Asia Design Awards, Best Book Design at South Korea's Paju Book Award, and Prize Nominee Works from the Tokyo Type Directors Club Annual Awards.

PP. 079, 144-147

Ward Roberts
ward-roberts.com

Ward Roberts is an independent conceptual artist in New York who creates exquisitely composed photographs drawing on themes such as the effects of loneliness and isolation in the modern world. His fresh and engaging perspective involves contradicting a sophisticated aesthetic with subtle unscripted moments.

PP. 600-609

Werklig
werklig.com

Werklig is a Finnish design agency that helps brands become meaningful. Underlined by a belief in sound reasoning and longevity through authenticity, it goes beyond the surface to build better narratives, relationships, and businesses.

PP. 148-151

Weston Doty
behance.net/westond

Weston Doty studied at the Savannah College of Art and Design (SCAD), majoring in graphic design. Through photography, collage, and illustration, his work explores the use of colour throughout a variety of different mediums.

PP. 558-565

Where's Gut Studio
wheresgut.com

Founded by Magdalene Wong, Where's Gut is a graphic design studio named after its resident cat and a word that means 'luck' and 'tangerine' in Cantonese. It uses strategic storytelling to achieve practical solutions that are timeless and engaging, underlined by a belief in sustainable and human-centred designs that support important issues.

PP. 310-313

Wonmin Park Studio
wonminpark.com

Wonmin Park is an artist who has shown in major museums and fairs around the world. He works with resin to produce a surreal, dream-like quality reminiscent of seeing something without fixed contours – bound together by light and air. After working with a few design companies in The Netherlands, he established his eponymous Eindhoven-based studio in 2011.

PP. 542-547

WV Design Studio
wvdesign.kr

WV Design is a Seoul-based design studio founded by Chae Won-Sik and Kim Bo-Ryung. Since 2013, it has been working on design projects across various mediums, ranging from furniture and products to brand identities. In exploring attractive results, it always places appeal over perfection.

PP. 530-535

Acknowledgements

We would like to specially thank all the designers
and studios who are featured in this book for their
significant contribution towards its compilation.
We would also like to express our deepest gratitude
to our producers for their invaluable advice and
assistance throughout this project, as well as the
many professionals in the creative industry who were
generous with their insights, feedback, and time.
To those whose input was not specifically credited or
mentioned here, we truly appreciate your support.

Future Editions

If you wish to participate in viction:ary's future projects
and publications, please send your portfolio to:
we@victionary.com